Zen
and
Japanese Buddhism

" Eka Offering His Severed Arm to Bodhidharma as a Pledge "

(Frontispiece)

(Painted on paper in *sumi* ink and tinted lightly. Treasure of the Sainenji Temple, Aichi Prefecture. Registered as an "Important Cultural Property.")

This masterpiece by Sesshu, well-known painter of the 15th century, relates an episode in the life of Bodhidharma (pp. 18 & 23).

The picture shows the high moment when Eka, later successor of Bodhidharma in China, exposes his left arm, which he has severed by his own sword to show his fervent desire to become a disciple of the great Bodhidharma, who in his meditations at first coldly disregards Eka's earnest request. However, finally moved by Eka's sincerity, Bodhidharma accepts him as a disciple.

(See overleaf for caption)

Zen

and
Japanese Buddhism

Daisetz Teitaro Suzuki

Munshiram Manoharlal
Publishers Pvt. Ltd.

ISBN 81-215-0966-1

This edition 2000
Originally published in 1958
Published with the permission of the original publisher
© 2000, Munshiram Manoharlal Publishers Pvt. Ltd., New Delhi

Printed and published by
Munshiram Manoharlal Publishers Pvt. Ltd.,
Post Box 5715, 54 Rani Jhansi Road,
New Delhi 110 055.

PREFACE

No thoughtful foreign visitors to Japan will be satisfied with mere sightseeing. They will naturally like to see into the moral and spiritual background of Japanese life and culture,—which means getting acquainted with Buddhism. For Buddhism has given to Japan, besides its spiritual outlook, its arts, philosophy, literature, architecture, morality, and many other things.

The best way to see the influence of Buddhism on Japanese culture, in its various manifestations, would be to wipe out all the Buddhist temples together with their treasures, libraries, gardens, anecdotes, tales, and romances of various sorts, and see what would be left in the cultural history of Japan and also in the present life of the people. No paintings, no sculptures, no architectural works, no music, no dramas, —this would be the state of affairs, not to speak of the disappearance of the minor branches of art such as landscape gardening, the art of tea, flower-arrangement, swordplay, etc. The handicraft arts to which Buddhism gave its first impetus would also have vanished.

Prince Shōtoku Taishi (574–622), who was the great patron and scholar of Buddhism when it was first introduced to Japan from the Asiatic continent, is still worshipped by carpenters and architects as their guardian saint; it is a well-known fact that anything approaching architecture in Japan dates from the erection of Hōryūji by this wonderful personage in the year 607 A.D. The temple is a grand ensemble of buildings still standing in Nara, the ancient capital of Japan.

The origin of Japanese education is traceable to the colleges established in connection with Hōryūji and Kōfukuji, though plans for general education were not worked out in Japan until the time when Kōbō Daishi (774–835), one of the greatest Buddhists, founded his school known as "Shugei Shuchi-In" in 828. Various social-welfare undertakings including the hospital, the bathhouse, the botanical garden, "herb hunting," and other activities all owe their existence to the efforts of early Buddhists in the seventh century and after.

It was again due to the initiative of those indefatigable Buddhist monks who traveled throughout Japan in the early days of Buddhism for the propagation of their faith that mountains were climbed, rivers bridged, roads built, fields tilled, wells dug, hot springs explored, trees planted, and canals opened for irrigation. Travelers in Japan, even in the remotest parts of the country, come across some legends in which Buddhist names are connected with the sacred straw ropes, or some curiously-shaped stones, etc. The names of Gyōgi Bosatsu (668–749) and Kōbō Daishi are to be mentioned in this connection.

Of all the Buddhist sects or schools, including those developed in Japan such as the Nichiren and the Shin, the Zen is to be singled out as a unique spiritual force that contributed so much to the formation of Japanese culture and character ever since its introduction to Japan in the thirteenth century under the Hōjō government. Let me quote Sir George B. Sansom, who writes in his *Japan* (first edition, p. 329):

> And there is one respect in which their (Japanese) religious history is probably unique, namely the development of the Zen sect. The influence of this school upon Japan has been so subtle and pervading that it has become the essence of her finest culture. To follow its ramifications in thought and sentiment, in art, letters and behaviour, would be to write exhaustibly the most difficult and the most fascinating chapter of her spiritual history...

All this will not be disputed by writers on the cultural history of the Japanese people.

A knowledge of Buddhism, therefore, not only in its general features but in some cases in its specific aspects as related to Japanese culture, is very much desired. It goes without saying that the geographical and political knowledge alone of the country and its people does not exhaust Japan.

The first edition of *Japanese Buddhism* was published in 1938. After the War general interest in Japanese culture with all its manifold efflorescence seems to have increased, especially in the Zen form of Buddhism, and the Japan Travel Bureau has asked me to write a separate chapter on Zen for the second edition of the book. When I finished, the work turned out to be much longer than I had first planned.

It was suggested that Zen might make an independent brochure. After some deliberation we have come to the conclusion that Zen and Japanese Buddhism should go together but with Zen first, for various reasons, which need not be enumerated here. Most of the illustrations were supplied through the kindness of Professor Shōkin Furuta and Mr. Hisatoyo Ishida of the Tokyo National Museum.

Cambridge, Massachusetts
February, 1958

D. T. S.

CONTENTS

ILLUSTRATIONS

PART I

ZEN BUDDHISM

I

WHAT IS ZEN?
NOT DHYANA BUT PRAJNA

1

Zen is a school of Buddhism which developed, or, it may be better to say, originated in China. While its philosophical roots are no doubt in India, its moral and psychological trunks could never have attained their fullest maturity except on Chinese soil. For in Zen we find what is characteristic of the Chinese mentality and which can be expressed most effectively in the Chinese language. Though the term *zen* or *zenna* (*ch'an* or *ch'anna* in Chinese) is the transliterated form of the Sanskrit *dhyāna,* it is far from emphasizing *dhyāna.* Its pivotal teachings are rather to be found in *bodhi* and *prajñā* and *anābhogacaryā.*

Dhyāna is generally translated as "meditation," or "a concentrated state of consciousness," whereas what Zen proposes is not to make us realize this, but to bring about the awakening of a higher spiritual power so as to come directly in contact with reality itself. This power, called *prajñā* in Sanskrit and transcribed in Chinese as *pan-jou* and in Japanese as *hannya,* is the highest form of intuition we humans are in possession of. By the exercise of *prajñā*-intuition, we attain what is known as *bodhi* in Sanskrit, *puti* in Chinese, *bodai* in Japanese. *Bodhi,* or more fully *sambodhi,* is "the supreme enlightenment" which was attained by Gautama when he was sitting cross-legged under the bodhi-tree by the river Nairañjanā in the northern part of

[3]

India, about twenty-five centuries ago. After this, Gautama, son of Śuddhodana, came to be known as Buddha, the Enlightened One.

It is for this reason that Buddhism is now known as a religion of enlightenment, based on the personal experience of the Buddha. And this experience is not the sole possession of the founder of Buddhism, for every devout spirit who would understand the Buddhist teaching and practice it as it is taught is sure to experience an enlightenment essentially the same as Buddha's and be above the concatenation of causes and effects, that is, beyond the cosmic net of karmic relationship. Therefore, Buddhism is also said to be a religion of emancipation and freedom.

A life of emancipation which results from the experience of enlightenment means that one is free from the bondage of karmic causation, or that one has crossed the stream of birth-and-death (*saṃsāra*) to the other side, to nirvana.

While such terms as emancipation, freedom, and nirvana may be taken as simply negativistic and having nothing positive and constructive, we must not forget the fact that these terms are only relative and in themselves have no final meaning. Because of our feeling bound by birth and death or good and evil or truth and falsehood, we speak of our being emancipated or freed or abiding in nirvana. Language is a treacherous instrument we invented when we desired to communicate our experiences. Instead of conveying exactly and truthfully what we have experienced, it is always liable to make us take the symbol for reality. For instance, when we talk of nirvana we imagine that there is such a thing called nirvana as in the case of a table or a book.

Front view of a hall for *zazen,* religious meditation.

LIFE AT A ZEN MONKS' TRAINING SCHOOL

"As Zen aims at attaining enlightenment or experiencing awakening, it has a number of training schools organized for the purpose. They are called 'Semmon Dōjō' or simply 'Sōdō' or 'Zendō.' The monks and laymen who wish to study Zen come here and go through several years of hard training." Each of the three Zen schools, the Rinzai, Sōtō and Ōbaku, though having the same goal in *zazen* has its own way of practicing it, which differs in some points from the others.

The series of photographs presented here (pp. 5 to 16) to illustrate the austerities practiced in Zen were, with the exception of the one on page 6 showing two monks at a temple entrance, taken specially for this book at the Engakuji, noted monastery of the Rinzai School of Zen Buddhism, at Kamakura, a tourist resort near Tokyo.

(Left) Two Zen monks on their peregrinations to find a master who will best lead them to enlightenment. The bundles which they carry in front and behind, suspended from their necks, contain all their personal effects. (This photo was taken at the Eiheiji, one of the two main temples of the Sōtō school.)

(Below) Here is a student monk awaiting admission to a "Semmon Dōjō." Often the students are obliged to remain at the entrance to the main hall of the "Semmon Dōjō" in this posture for at least two days, and sometimes even for a week, as a test of their earnestness, before their request is granted.

The four Chinese characters on the tablet over the entrance to this *zazen* hall signify that here Zen students undergo deep meditation in order that their inward eye may open and see the real truths of Buddhism.

(Above) Interior of the *zazen* hall. Each student has a space, three feet by six, assigned to him on an elevated platform, where he not only practices *zazen* but sleeps at night.

(Left) If any student during *zazen* should become drowsy or move about when his muscles grow cramped, or his attention should wander, the monk keeping watch will strike him sharply with a wooden stick, called a *keisaku*.

At fixed intervals during *zazen,* the students walk about, either in the *zazen* hall or outside, for a given length of time to relieve physical numbness.

On a certain day of the month the students go out on a round of alms begging, which is also a means of mental training. Each carries a bag suspended from the neck in which to receive the coins or rice that may be given him as alms. The alms they receive are added to their provisions or help to defray the expenses of their living.

The students usually sleep from nine at night till three in
the morning. The more ardent ones will often get up at
night to practice *zazen* out of doors, under the eaves of
a temple building, under the trees in the nearby woods, or
sometimes on a rock.

Twice a day the students see their master in his room to give him their answers to the *kōan* he has given them, and to ask what he has to say about their answers (p. 36). For this purpose they go in turn out of the *zazen* hall through the front entrance. Before entering their master's room they strike the small bell in the anteroom, which corresponds to knocking at the door.

Once a day the master reads the Zen classics to the students. In his lecture he tells them his own experiences, which he believes will help the students to attain *satori*, or enlightenment.

The Zen religion teaches that 'no work' means 'no food.' The students daily sweep the garden, clean the *zazen* hall, cook their own meals (composed chiefly of vegetables grown by themselves), and perform many other necessary tasks. They have meals twice a day as a rule—in the morning and at noon. Their breakfast consists of rice gruel and pickles,

their lunch of rice boiled with barley, *miso* (soy bean paste) soup, and pickles. No meat is taken. The evening meal, if taken at all, is regarded as a sort of medicine and consists of leftovers from lunch. Complete silence is kept during the meal time. Before and after each meal a selection from the scriptures is chanted solemnly.

The beginning, as well as the end, of each task in the students' daily routine is announced by striking with a mallet the flat wooden block hanging near the front entrance to the *zazen* hall. On this block are written words cautioning the students not to develop the habits of negligence and laziness.

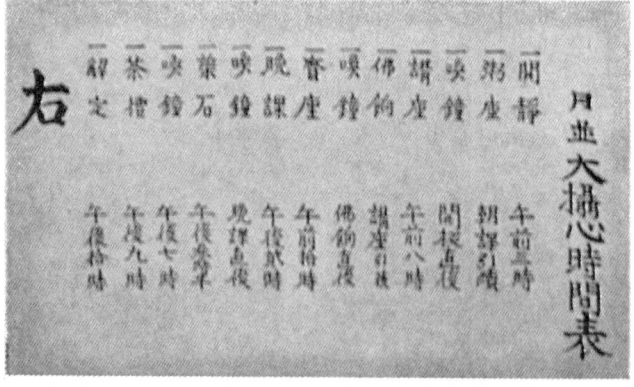

Daily schedule for one week of intensive training each month during which students must rise at three in the morning and sit in meditation until ten at night.

Nirvana, however, is no more than a state of mind or consciousness when we actually transcend relativity—the world of birth-and-death.

Therefore, nirvana is not a special world set above this world of opposites. If it is so we are creating a new pair of opposites, with nirvana on one side and birth-and-death on the other. There would then be no transcendence. Nirvana is birth-and-death and birth-and-death is nirvana. When this identification is reached there is a transcendence. This is called *anābhogacaryā* from the psychological-metaphysical point of view. *Anābhogacaryā* means a life of purposelessness, a life of filling up the well with snow.

When Buddha was about to pass away after forty-nine years of missionary activity in the northern parts of India, he is recorded to have declared: "All these forty-nine years I have not spoken a word on the Dharma*." This is Buddha's life of *anābhogacaryā,* given expression from what we may call a dialectical point of view. As a matter of fact Buddha's life was full of giving oral or verbal instructions to his numerous disciples, who later compiled what is known as the *tripitaka,* "three baskets of Buddhist literature": *sūtra, vinaya,* and *abhidharma,*** which according to Chinese estimates comprise more than five thousand volumes. If this

---

* Truth, Reality, the Absolute From the *Lankāvatāra Sūtra.*

** (1) The *sūtra* is the collection of Buddha's sermons, discourses, dialogues, etc., compiled by his immediate disciples after his death. (2) The *vinaya* is the collection of moral precepts given by Buddha to his disciples and lay devotees. (3) The *abhidharma* contains mostly philosophical works written by Buddha's chief disciples explaining his teachings.

is the case, how could Buddha make the announcement "not a word uttered"? This, however, is no less than an utterance directly expressing at least one aspect of his enlightenment-experience, and it is here that Zen claims its reason of being.

I am afraid I have somewhat digressed, but from the above statements it will be clear that Zen Buddhism, while it has not severed itself from practicing *dhyāna,* puts its principal emphasis on attaining enlightenment, thus following Buddha's example as well as his teaching. *Dhyāna* practice is no doubt an important step towards the enlightenment-experience, but Zen Buddhism does not believe that it is the only approach to the final goal of all Buddhist discipline.

2

According to the traditional records upheld by Chinese Zen followers, Bodhidharma, who came to China from India in 527 A.D., is regarded as the first patriarch of Zen in China. But in reality the Zen school of Buddhism started with the sixth patriarch, Enō (Hui-nêng, died 713), who for the first time laid a firm foundation for the idea that the Buddhist life consists in awakening *prajñā*-intuition and not in disciplining oneself in *dhyāna* exclusively.

The following four lines are generally considered as summing up the essence of Zen Buddhism:

A special transmission outside the doctrinal teaching:

No dependence on letters or words,
Pointing directly at the Mind in every one of us,
And seeing into one's Nature, whereby one attains
    Buddhahood.

It is not known exactly when and by whom this *gātha* of four lines was composed. Perhaps it began to circulate among Zen followers sometime after the rise of Enō (Hui-nêng), the sixth patriarch of Zen, because Enō does not seem to have been acquainted with this slogan. His pronouncement, which was made while under Gunin (Hung-jên, 602–75), known as the fifth patriarch of Zen in China, runs as follows:

Bodhi (enlightenment) has from the first nothing to
    do with the tree,
The bright mirror has also no stand on which to
    place itself.
The Buddha-nature is eternally illuminating,
And where could dust ever accumulate?*

This was against Jinshū's** (Shên-hsiu, died 706) standpoint:

---

* These lines are taken from the work known as "The Sixth Patriarch's Platform Sūtra" (*Rokuso Dangyō, Liu-tsu Tan-ching*), excavated at Tun-huang more than fifty years ago. The later editions of the text have for the third line: "There is from the first not one thing." I do not know how this variation or alteration came to take place.
** Jinshū was the foremost disciple of Gunin, who is said to have had more than one thousand followers.

The body is the Bodhi-tree,
The Mind is like a bright mirror.
Keep it clean all the time,
And let not dust accumulate.

Now, Jinshū was a great scholar as contrasted with the reported illiteracy of Enō, the son of a poor peasant. The latter was not even a regularly ordained monk, he was simply one of the lay-brothers working in the back-yard of the monastery. Jinshū advocated learning and the practice of *dhyāna* as a necessary means leading to the attainment of the highest experience, whereas Enō was not necessarily an opponent of the *dhyāna* discipline, but he asserted the all-importance of *prajñā*-intuition, which directly enters into the heart of the Buddhist life. Jinshū thought that the Mind was to be kept free from the dust of the defiling passions so that the ultimate reality would be reflected on it in the way a brightly-shining mirror will truthfully reflect images of all things brought before it. The Mind-mirror, according to Jinshū, was something which was liable to be stained by external objects and had to be guarded jealously against this possibility. Enō's experience, however, was contrary to this, for he found the Mind-mirror forever in a state of purity and absolutely beyond the possibility of defilement by external agencies. He even went further, declaring that there was from the very beginning nothing to be described as a brightly-illuminating Mind-mirror. In fact, his negativism was most thoroughgoing, but this did not of course mean that Enō advocated absolute nihilism. His was, if we can at all give it a name, a form of transcendentalism. Buddhists call it the doctrine of "emptiness" (*śūnyatā* in Sanskrit). It belongs in the realm transcending all forms of relativity. Relativity characterizes the world we humans inhabit, while Emptiness, though not outside this world, is to be distinguished from it in so far as we, being social beings desiring in every possible way to communicate our experiences, have to use language. Unfortunately, we have not yet succeeded in designing a perfect means of communication, subjectively and objectively. The outcome is that Zen often remains silent, or utters incoherent sounds, and wants its students to understand what they mean. Hence its claim for "a special transmission outside the doctrinal teaching, and no dependence on words or letters."

"Emptiness" is a metaphysical term, and the followers of Zen generally speak of "Mind" or "Nature" as they are more concerned with individual personality. They identify the Emptiness with the Mind or the Nature (or the Buddha-nature). "Directly pointing at the Mind," therefore, means taking hold of it by means of *prajñā*-intuition, though there is nothing really to take hold of as "Mind." Mind is no-mind and it is out of this no-mind that the whole panorama, infinitely rich in content, of the relative world unrolls itself.

3

Enō's discovery of no-mind (*mushin*) as the psychological equivalent for the Emptiness which is attained by the awakening of *prajñā*-intuition paved the way to a further broadening of the field of consciousness. For the no-mind dives into the deepest recesses of our being, it is infinitely deeper than what is generally designated as the unconscious. The psychologist's unconscious is part of consciousness. Though superficially and by definition it denies consciousness, it by no means implies that it is something altogether different in nature from consciousness so called. The unconscious is at the furthest end of consciousness but not outside it, while the no-mind belongs in an altogether different category. It is what makes up both the conscious and the unconscious, it is in them, with them, but it is more than both of them; it is more fundamental. For this reason, the no-mind is an inexhaustible reservoir of possibilities. When it is tapped, our consciousness gains power in various ways: ethically, aesthetically, intellectually, and emotionally.

Prior to Enō, *dhyāna* appeared somehow separated from *prajñā*. Though *prajñā* was not ignored by any means, the successive patriarchs seemed to put stress unwittingly upon *dhyāna* in accordance with the Indian tradition. In truth they never neglected *prajñā*, only they did not so expressively, so consciously, so decisively, insist upon the all-importance of *prajñā* in connection with *dhyāna*.

Bodhidharma's "wall-gazing" (J. *hekikan*; C. *pi-kuan*) was thought to be a model pattern of meditation posture. Although what he was really emphasizing has nothing to do with the physical side of the *dhyāna* exercise, nor with the encouragement of *dhyāna* alone at the expense of *prajñā*-intuition, some of his followers took Bodhidharma's "wall-gazing" to suit their own one-sided interpretation. The passage relating to this part of Bodhidharma's teaching is as follows:

> By "Entrance by Reason" we mean the realization of the spirit of Buddhism by the aid of the scriptural teaching. We then come to have a deep faith in the True Nature which is one and the same in all sentient beings. The reason why it does not manifest itself is the overwrapping of external objects and false thoughts. When one, abandoning the false and embracing the true, in simpleness of thought, abides in *pi-kuan,* one finds that there is neither selfhood nor otherness, that the masses and the worthies are of one essence. He firmly holds to this belief and never moves away from it. He will not then be guided by any literary instructions, for he is in silent communion with the Truth itself, free from conceptual discriminations, serene and not-acting. This is called "Entrance by Reason."*

The following is the view of Dōshin (Tao-hsin), the fourth patriarch, (580–651), as regards the qualification of a *dhyāna* master:

> He is one who is not annoyed by quietude or by confusion. Such is a person who likes *dhyāna* and keeps his mind on guard. When the mind is made always to abide in *śamatha* (quieting) it sinks into torpidity; when it is for a long time employed in

---

* D. T. Suzuki, *Essays in Zen Buddhism,* Series I (London: Rider, 1950), pp. 178–9.

vipaśyanā (contemplation), it is subject to frustration. In the *Lotus Sūtra* we have: "Buddha himself abides in the Mahayana and in accordance with the Dharma in which he has adorned himself with the power of *dhyāna* and *prajñā,* and thereby helps all beings to cross the stream of *saṃsāra.*"*

"The Dharma adorned with *dhyāna* and *prajñā*" is significant. The fourth patriarch must be said to have thoroughly understood how the teaching and discipline of Zen Buddhism were to be oriented. The sixth patriarch was most explicit in identifying *dhyāna* and *prajñā* and, if anything, placed *prajñā* more in the forefront. This was unmistakably seen in Jinne (Shên-hui, died 706), one of the foremost disciples of Enō, when he declared that "to know (*chih*) is the portal to all mysteries." "To know (*chih*)" here of course means the awakening of *prajñā*.

The answer of Dōshin, the fourth patriarch, to the following question will help clarify his relationship to Enō, the sixth patriarch: "How can one by having an insight into the nature of the Dharma attain to clearness and purity of mind?"

Dōshin answered: "No invoking the Buddha's name, no trying to seize upon the mind, no contemplation on the mind, no deliberation, no speculation, no concentration, no scattering of thought; only let things flow on as they would,

---

* This is from Jōkaku (Ching-chiao) in his *Masters and Disciples of the Lankāvatāra,* (J. *Ryōga Shijiki;* C. *Leng-ch'ieh Shih-tzu Chi*), one of the T'ang MSS excavated at Tun-huang about sixty years ago.

Tokyo National Museum

"Hui-nĕng Cutting a Bamboo Stalk"—a picture by Liang-kai (p. 34) in which the master himself shares in the general work of the monastery, illustrating the importance of manual labor in Zen training. (Painted in *sumi* ink on paper. Owned by the Tokyo National Museum.)

"Byakue Kannon (White-robed Goddess of Mercy) Sitting
on a Rock by a River," by Mu-chi (p. 34). (Painted in *sumi*
ink on paper. Treasure of Daitokuji Temple, Kyoto City.)

neither let them pass away, nor let them stay on; be one, be alone, clean of all appendages, and ultimately the mind will all by itself be clear and unspoiled."*

This state of mind is echoed by Enō, the sixth patriarch, when he tells us to realize "no-mind," "no-form," and "no-abiding," and further advises us "to keep Tao (i.e., *prajñā*) ever flowing with no obstructions." This keeping the stream of consciousness in a state of constant flowing without any kind of interruption or interference external or internal is the working of *prajñā* and the ultimate goal of Zen discipline. The technical name given this discipline is *ekākāra-samādhi* or *ekalaksha-samādhi* (J. *ichigyō-sammai*; C. *i-hsing-san-mei*), that is, "concentration exercise in one-ness." This is defined by Enō as disciplining oneself in straightforwardness, or single-mindedness, or in cultivating the mind-in-itself-ness. When a man has no attachment to any object (*dharma*), is altogether free, and, by giving up all delusive ways of thinking, follows the mind as it moves on in accordance to its native laws—that is, when the mind harbors no crookedness in it, when it does not violate its own nature, when it finds no hindrances as it flows on in obedience to the order inherent to it—then the discipline in the *samādhi* of oneness is brought to its final stage of fruition, which is also known as *anābhogacaryā*, life of no-merit or purposelessness. A Zen master once remarked, "The solid rock does not permit even a pin-head to enter." To challenge this another master declared, "I plant a flower on the rock."

---

* *Ibid.*

II

THE DEVELOPMENT OF ZEN

Zen flourished in China throughout the T'ang (616–905) and the Sung (960–1278) and the Yüan (1206–1314) dynasties and began to decline in the Ming dynasty (1368–1628). What Zen did in China during this long period may be summed up as follows:

(1) The Zen followers adapted Zen to the Chinese psychology, which means that Buddhism, out of which Zen developed, ceased to be a foreign importation. Zen began to talk directly to the people in their own language instead of resorting to the difficult abstract conceptualization customary in Indian thought. It is in Zen literature that the dialects of the T'ang dynasty are preserved. Before the sixth patriarch, Buddhism still retained a great many Indian philosophical terms which were not easy for the ordinary people to understand and digest in their everyday life.

(2) Zen brought the abstraction down to earth. Buddha was not only the enlightened one with all the marks of great manhood but, also, a mere blade of grass torn into pieces by a breath of wind. He was also the bridge over the mountain-stream at the Jōshū (Chao-chou) monastery, which was trodden over rudely by every passer-by, including horses and donkeys.

(3) Zen was demonstrated wherever the monks were,

reading the sutras or visiting a family in mourning or picking tea-leaves in the garden. Hō Koji (Pang Chü-shih), the lay Zen-man of the T'ang dynasty, sang:

How miraculous, how wonderful!

I draw water, I carry wood!

When a master was walking with a disciple in the deserted fields, the latter asked, "Could the Buddha-dharma be found in this wilderness?" Said the master, "How big this rock and how small that stone!"

The daughter of Hō, the lay Zen-man, was also a Zen follower. When she was gathering some herbs in the field, Tanka (Tan-hsia, 738–824), a good friend of her father's, passed by and asked for her father, saying, "Where is he?" The maiden put down on the ground the basket she was carrying and stood with her hands folded over her chest. Tanka, as if not observing her, repeated, "Where is your father?" She now took up the basket and walked away.

(4) Hyakujō (Pao-chang, died 814) was the founder of a new type of Buddhist monastery in China, for he found that Zen life could not be carried out in the older system. The new order was a self-supporting and self-governing body. It was divided into several departments such as treasury, ceremonies, culinary, provisions, farming, etc. Each department had its office headed by an elder monk and assisted by younger ones. When the whole Brotherhood was engaged for instance in the field, the master himself came out to work with the rest. While working in this way, the master and disciples would engage in a demonstration of Zen. Book-reading or studying the classical literature was not the sole means of acquiring Buddha-knowledge, nor was

sitting cross-legged in the Meditation Hall the most efficient method of getting enlightened. Zen was in the monk's moving his limbs, carrying food to his mouth, responding to the calls of nature, answering the master's summons, etc. Zen was not beyond his everyday life, it was in great events as well as in minor deeds. The monks never despised menial labor; nothing was below their dignity, for Zen is life itself.

(5) What might be called religious peregrination was a custom among Zen monks all over the country. As Zen spread over the kingdom, monasteries were built in the mountainous regions. The larger ones are recorded to have harbored more than a thousand monks. They peregrinated from one monastery to another during a certain season of the year. The idea was to find the master who would best help lead them to enlightenment. Each master had his own pedagogic methodology which appealed more readily to certain monks than others. The master, too, realized this, and often would advise his pupils to go somewhere else where he thought they would fare better, for the master's personal character frequently has much to do with the spiritual development of his disciples. This is psychologically inevitable. The peregrination, covering a large area inhabited by villagers and townspeople, afforded fine opportunities to get acquainted with all classes and all types of human beings, and must have been a real education for the monks in a variety of senses. Thus equipped with rich experience not only in Zen but in all human affairs and relationships, the monks completed their character training and naturally invited the respect and confidence of the people generally,

though the monks themselves were indifferent to worldly considerations. In the heyday of the T'ang and the Sung dynasties, when Zen most flourished, it was in its monasteries that great moral and intellectual characters of the time found their shelter.

(6) The development of what is known as neo-Confucianism in the Sung dynasty owes much to the influence of Zen thought. Zen has not much to do with thought as such, but it was natural that some of the philosophically-minded Zen masters would do a great deal of philosophical thinking about the experiences they had accumulated during their long study of Zen as a discipline in enlightenment. This was partly brought about by Zen's affiliation with the philosophy of Kegon (*Hua-yen* in Chinese, *Avatamsaka* or *Gandhavyūha* in Sanskrit). The Kegon school marks the highest point in the systematization of Buddhist thought as it presented itself to the Chinese mind during the Sui and the T'ang dynasties. It was led by such intellectual giants as Tojun (Tu-shun, 556–640), Chigon (Chih-yen, 602–68), and Hōzō (Fatsang, 643–713). Even the Confucians, who generally looked upon foreign thought as not suited to the Chinese way of living, could not resist visiting the Zen monasteries and studying what was going on inside them. The Confucians found the Buddhist philosophy too alluring for the intellectuals not to come in touch with and finally to be made captive by it.

(7) Life in the monastery was minutely and strictly defined, and the monks were expected to observe all the rules conscientiously. The reason for this came from the Zen discipline that tends to latitudinarianism or antinomian-

ism. This was a most dangerous and most undesirable tendency in Zen. During the T'ang dynasty its devotees were often censored for not reading the sutras, not worshipping at the Buddha-shrine, not strictly observing the precepts, etc. There was a master who burned a Buddha-image to warm himself on a cold winter night; another caught a fish and ate it to keep himself alive; and still another drank intoxicating liquor and afterwards was never seen sober. These examples were not necessarily rare events. Superficially their deeds were surely inexcusable. And then there was perhaps in the Zen teaching of Emptiness a tendency to justify misdemeanors because Emptiness was something transcending worldly considerations or moral conventionalities. The masters were very much against all such abnormalities. Telling their pupils not to deviate from the prevailing ideas of decorum or decency, they put them under an exacting discipline. In the Sung dynasty Zen monks' behavior once won the warmest appraisal of distinguished Confucian dignitaries who happened to visit a Zen monastery.

(8) Confucianism is no doubt the philosophy of the Chinese people; it is the product of their psychology and perfectly fits their taste and their way of thinking and living. Taoism represented by Lao-tzu and Chuang-tzu also came out of the Chinese mind, but I am inclined to think its appeal is to a minority and perhaps to somewhat eccentrically disposed intellectuals. An overwhelming majority of the people side with Confucius and his teachings. They like dignity, decorum, stately behavior; they are given to *li* (J. *rei*) and *yüeh* (J. *gaku*), rites and music, whereas

Taoist thinking when wrongly applied is liable to be libertinistic. As we see especially in the writings of Chuang-tzu, the Taoists were severe critics of the time, and tended to be escapists as well as free-thinking spirits. Freedom of thought and independence of spirit are refreshingly theirs. Confucians are upholders of conventional morality and of smooth and harmonious temperament. There is not in them much of revolution.

The Zen monks have more of independent thinking than of philistinism, and it is due to this independence on the part of Zen that Chinese thought was able to keep up its viability. The so-called dialectics of Zen is more to the point than the Taoists'. It is not at all veiled, it directly goes to its objectives and leaves no time for thought to vacillate or prevaricate. The master takes up his staff and demands, "I do not call it a staff and what do you call it? Speak, speak!" No answer comes, and he goes down from the pulpit and walks away with his staff. Zen is something which unexpectedly turns up in your way as if to attack you from ambush. You may have to be always on guard. Zen is in one way bewitching and this is the reason why the Sung philosophers often compared Zen to "enticing music and a coquettish woman." They apparently could not resist its magic-like fascination.

(9) Zen disregards conventionalism, ritualism, institutionalism, in fact anything that is binding and restricting. Zen stands for absolute freedom. This means that Zen comes out of the deepest sources of being where infinite possibilities are stored up. Zen dips its fingers into them and works out its inexhaustible creativity. In Sung following T'ang,

the Chinese mind was richly influenced by Zen, and what
may be designated the Zen style of painting, which refused
sheepishly to adapt itself to the classical traditionalism,
developed. It is Zen's privilege that it manages not to get into
the rut of just being ordinary. This of course does not mean
that it wants to deny or defy wantonly the reasonableness
of authoritarianism. It stands against the latter when indi-
viduality is unnecessarily trampled upon. Zen is not to be
thought rebellious in any circumstance. It is quite subservient
to authority and regimentalism when it sees their wisdom.
In this respect it closely allies itself with art. Art is one field
of human activity where originality and creativity are
freely asserted. This is seen in such works of art as produced
by Baen (Ma-yüan), Ryōkai (Liang-kai), Mokkei (Mu-chi),
and others of the Sung dynasty.

(10) As I said before, Zen brought God in Heaven down
onto the earth and also transferred the Pure Land, so many
millions of leagues away in the Western quarters, to this
land of patience and defilement (*sahaloka* in Sanskrit).
God ceased to be a something outside us and consequently
his kingdom was to be conceived as our own and its
inhabitants were no less than ourselves, including all that
makes up this universe. So with the Pure Land. We do
not have to travel such a long way to reach it, and this
after death. The Pure Land is right here with us, we
have always been in it. This idea of Zen has revolutionalized
our *welt-anschauung*. Nature with all that makes it up—
with beings sentient and non-sentient—was not something
to conquer and to be subjugated, but they were all our
friends and relatives who were to be cherished and beloved

and admired. Kannon (Kuan-yin, Avalokiteshvara), "Goddess of Mercy," was not to be kept enshrined somewhere in a sanctified locality; Monju (Wen-chu, Mañjuśrī), the Bodhisattva of Wisdom, was not to be imprisoned up at the summit of Mount Wutai. Both Kannon and Monju were brought down to the market or the woods or anywhere where we humans were accessible. Kannon was pictured with a basket filled with fish, Monju came out to our world accompanied by the monkey or the crane. Nature and human beings and deities or Bodhisattvas all became citizen of one great democratic community. Zen is the principle of freedom and democracy.

III

SCHOOLS OF ZEN

Zen Buddhism was divided into five schools towards the end of the T'ang dynasty, that is, in the tenth century, and two of the five survive, as representing the two main aspects of the Zen discipline. The two are Sōtō (Ts'ao-tung) and Rinzai (Lin-chi). The characteristics of the two schools came to a sharp differentiation during the Sung dynasty when the Sōtō was represented by Wanshi (Huang-chih, 1090–1157) and the Rinzai by Daie (Tai-hui, 1089–1163).

What is known as *kōan* (*kung-an*) methodology developed under Daie and Engo (Yuan-wu, 1566–1642), who was Daie's teacher. This is a sort of pedagogic device to help the Zen student come to an enlightenment experience. It generally comes in the form of a problem which he is told to solve cr answer. For instance:

"What is your original face which you have before your parents gave birth to you?"

"What is that which makes you answer when you are called?"

"When your corpse is cremated and the ashes are scattered to the winds, where are you?"

"When a master was asked whether or not the dog has Buddha-nature, he answered, '*Mu!*' (*wu* in Chinese), meaning, 'No!' What does this '*mu*' really mean?"

A modern Japanese Zen master called Hakuin used to

hold up his left hand and demand, "Hear the sound of one hand."

All these highly-metaphysical questions are given Zen students for solution. The solution, however, is not to be given along intellectual or conceptual lines, for in this case Zen will be no more than a philosophical exercise. What the master wants is to have you give him your inner intuitional understanding without resorting to any kind of verboseness.

This giving a *kōan* to the student to accelerate an intuitional understanding was considered by Wanshi, the chief opponent of Daie, to be too artificial, unnecessarily trying to speed the understanding (*satori* in Japanese). To do anything to speed or force *satori* was against the very reason of Zen. Zen, it was objected, wants us to experience the suchness or is-ness of things not only statically but dynamically. Being so, to lay schemes as regards this suchness is to prick the perfect skin of the healthy body, an altogether uncalled-for interference. Let suchness alone as it should be. This was the position taken by the Sōtō masters of the Sung dynasty. The Rinzai devotees called the latter followers of "silent illumination," implying that however long they may sit cross-legged waiting for suchness to present itself, this will never take place, inasmuch as they do not do anything active towards this end. Thus the feud between the Rinzai and the Sōtō has been going on ever since the days of Wanshi and Daie, who were the two great representative masters of the Sung dynasty.

As far as Zen itself is concerned, it always creates a situation whose evaluation is so upsetting for the uninitiated that they wonder how to deal with it. Are the masters playing with words? Are they really in earnest? Is Zen literature nothing but "a farrago of anecdotes reporting grotesque and irrelevant sayings and still more grotesque and often brutal actions"? Zen is really aggravating in more senses than one. Tokusan (Tê-shan, 782–865) used to say: "When you ask, you commit a fault; when you do not ask, you go against." A monk came forward and when he was about to make bows before the master, the master struck him. The monk protested, "I have not even asked you a question, so why should I be struck by you, O Master?" The master answered, "What is the use if I wait for you to speak?" This explains where Zen is. There is no need of talking about the difference between the Sōtō and the Rinzai schools.

The Rinzai school came to Japan with Eisai (1141–1215), who went to China first in 1168 and again in 1187. It was during his second visit that he studied Zen under Kyoan (Hsü-an). When Eisai came back in 1191, he determined to propagate Zen in Japan, but the opposition of the older school at Mount Hiei, northeast of Kyoto, was too strong and vehement. It was some time later (1202) that he succeeded in building a Zen temple in the capital, which, however, could not be exclusively devoted to the study of Zen. Eisai had to be conciliatory to the old school, which moved the Emperor to command Eisai to teach, also, some other branches of Buddhism. The exclusive Rinzai Zen teaching took place when Daiō Kokushi ("the national teacher," 1235–1308) and other promient monks came back from China and some of the Chinese masters came over to Japan—mostly in the latter part of the thirteenth century.

Wooden image of Eisai Zenji. (Carved in the 13th century.
Treasure of Jufukuji Temple, Kamakura City.)

Institute of Art Research

Portrait of Dōgen Zenji. (Painted in color on silk in the 13th century. Treasure of Hokyōji Temple, Fukui Prefecture.)

The Chinese priests were very much patronized by the Kamakura government (1192–1333), especially by the Hōjō family, and monasteries were built for them in Kamakura. The Japanese masters generally settled in Kyoto with their temples and monasteries well protected by the Imperial Court. When the Muromachi period (1393–1573) started in Kyoto, the capital turned into the headquarters of the Rinzai school of Zen.

The Kyoto Zen followers were well trained not only in Zen proper but in Confucian learning and also in secular affairs. They were thus active in business (especially in trading with China) and diplomacy and thereby the Ashikaga government was able to carry on its foreign policies with China.

The Zen monks were erudite scholars and artists. They printed many books on history, literature, and general culture, including books on Zen, Chinese and Japanese. They also helped the upper classes to appreciate the arts imported from China and thus stimulated the native artists to create their own. The Muromachi period, running from the latter part of the fourteenth century down to about the middle of the sixteenth, was one of the great periods in the cultural history of Japan. Zen played a most significant part in it.

The Sōtō school came to Japan in the Kamakura period when Dōgen (1200–53) returned from China after staying for over four years. While there were the "twenty-four streams" flowing between China and Japan for the Rinzai school before it got settled in Japan, the Sōtō was represented by Dōgen alone; there was no other line of transmission coming from China. The Japanese Sōtō school may thus better be called the Dōgen school. Indeed, Dogen is to his followers what Nichiren and Shinran and Hōnen are to their followers, that is to say, Dōgen is virtually the founder of the Sōtō school in Japan. This is partly due to Dōgen's having left a certain amount of writing for his disciples to follow. He was probably more philo-sophically-minded than his Rinzai colleagues. In China this was also the case. Tōzan (Tung-shan, 807–69), from whom the Sōtō school starts, had a speculative mind which led him to take up the study of Zen. When he was still very young he came, while reading one of the *Prajñāpāramitā Sūtras,* across the famous passage regarding "no eye, no ear, no nose, no tongue, no body, no mind"; he is said to have felt all over his face, and finding all his sense-organs perfect, he asked the teacher: "How could this passage be true? When the scripture is understood not to tell us anything that is not true, how does this wholesale denial go with the fact?" The doubt thus aroused plunged him into further pursuit of philosophical studies. Generally speaking, the Sōtō school shows a more speculative, meditative tempera-ment than the other schools.

The differences between the Rinzai and the Sōtō schools as they historically developed after their introduction to Japan may be described as follows:

(1) While Rinzai came in close relationship politically, economically, and culturally with the reigning families, Sōtō had its seats of study and training in the mountains remote from the center of political power. Dōgen hated to

approach people of influence and authority. When he was hard pressed by the Emperor to accept his gift of a purple robe, he acquiesced, but it is said that he never used it. The poem he composed at the time runs thus:

> While the valley of Eihei is shallow
> The Imperial command weighs heavy indeed.
> But the monkeys and the cranes may laugh
> At an old monk arrayed in purple.*

(2) The Sōtō school of Japan lays very much weight on the study of Dōgen's "Essays" as well as on sitting quietly facing the wall. The collection of Dōgen's "Essays" written in Japanese and numbering ninety-five is somewhat difficult reading, principally because of its peculiar style, altogether unique, defying tradition and imitation.

The Rinzai school, on the other hand, studies the Chinese Zen texts, especially the *Sayings of Rinzai (Lin-chi-lu)*, the *Hekigan-shū (Piyen-chi, The Blue Rock Collection)*, and the *Kai-an-koku Go (Words from Dream-land)* written by Daitō Kokushi and commented on by Hakuin (1685–1768). The last is a joint work by a Japanese master of the fourteenth century and another of the eighteenth century. The Rinzai monks devote themselves to the solution of *kōan*

---

* This is a literal translation of Dōgen's poem in Chinese. "Shallow" means that Dōgen's mountain-shelter is not situated very far away from human habitations. "Shallow" contrasts with "heavy." The valley is inhabited by the wild animals of nature such as monkeys and cranes. They are not tainted by human greed and are his good friends. Would they not laugh at an old rustic monk if he is seen in a purple robe which belongs to worldly power?

as was illustrated before. The *kōan* system of realizing *satori* and clarifying its contents step by step was perfected in Japan by Hakuin and his followers. The Rinzai in Japan is thus now practically the Hakuin school, for there are no Rinzai Zen masters in Japan who do not follow the pedagogic methodology initiated by this great teacher of Zen. While this has some weaknesses, it has helped to keep the study of Zen alive so far in the Far East.

(3) There are two main branches of the Sōtō school in Japan, the Eiheiji and the Sōjiji, which are united under one governing body. The Rinzai is divided into fourteen branches and each one of them has its own administrative body.

There are 15,190 temples under the Sōtō and 5,966 temples and monasteries under the Rinzai. There is another branch of Zen in Japan which is known as the Ōbaku. But this branch has nothing to do with the doctrine of Zen. The main temple, called Mampukuji, was built early in the Edo period, 1659, for a Chinese Zen monk who came to Japan. The temple is in the vicinity of Kyoto. It is built after the Chinese style and follows Chinese usages in its ritualistic performances. It has 503 temples under its jurisdiction.

Tokyo National Museum

"Tung-shan Crossing a River," by Ma-yüan (p. 34). It is said that Tung-shan, founder of the Sōtō school of Zen Buddhism, attained enlightenment when, crossing a river one day, he chanced to see his own reflection in the water. (Painted in color on silk. Owned by the Tokyo National Museum.)

Self-portrait of Hakuin. (Painted in *sumi* ink on paper. Owned by Mr. Moritatsu Hosokawa.)

IV

THE SATORI-EXPERIENCE

Zen has played a unique part in the cultural history of Japan. What the late Sir Charles Eliot says on this point is no exaggeration: "...perhaps it may not be amiss to point out once more how great a power it [Zen] has been in the artistic, intellectual, and even the political life of the Far East. To a certain extent it has molded the Japanese character. No other form of Buddhism is so thoroughly Japanese."*

The element in Zen that has achieved such an important influence in the molding of Japanese life is what is known as *satori*. *Satori* constitutes the essence of Zen, for where there is no *satori* there cannot be any form of Zen. Zen revolves around this axial experience.

What then is the *satori*-experience which has such a weighty significance in Zen and characterized the whole trend of Japanese culture? *Satori* is generally translated as "enlightenment," but "awakening" may be a better term. It is both noetic and affective. It is in fact to make an opening to our most fundamental mental activity—the activity which has not yet differentiated itself into anything to be definitively called this or that. When *satori* is experienced, something far more basic than either intellect or feeling is brought

---

* *Japanese Buddhism*, p. 396.

forward into the field of consciousness, though not in its relative sense. The psychologist has not yet given it any specific name, for this event transcends the psychology whose study does not go beyond what can be intellectually handled or scientifically measured. If I say that *satori* is the awakening of consciousness from the darkness of blind strivings, the psychologist will not understand it.

But as long as *satori* explores and reveals the deepest and darkest recesses of consciousness which have hitherto escaped our ordinary inspections or introspections, it is enlightenment. The reason why "awakening" is more appropriate than "enlightenment" to describe the nature of *satori*-experience is that while enlightenment is a static state of consciousness, awakening is a process which instantly brightens up the field of consciousness like a flash of lightning, though this does not mean that the consciousness thus once illuminated goes back to its former drabness. If this is the case it will be like the door which closes as soon as it opens. The *satori*-experience is not of this kind. The door once opened remains open. The vista once revealed to the person will not vanish away. But as it does not belong in the category of relativity, it is not at all communicable in any ordinary logical way.

In this connection, Sir Charles quotes William James: "This incommunicableness of the transport is the keynote of all mysticism."* *Satori* is no doubt incommunicable, but it is not any sort of transport. If it is, it will be a mere psy-

---

* *Varieties of Religious Experience,* p. 396. London: Longmans, Green & Co.

chological phenomenon and cannot have any deeper import. But it really is what stands at the basis of every philosophical system. It thus has a metaphysical connotation. *Satoru,* which is the verbal form of *satori,* is synonymous with *sameru,* which means "to wake" from a sleep or torpor. *Satori* in this sense is the act of awakening itself and not the state of consciousness *satori* makes one acquainted with. As to incommunicableness, nothing that enters into the very constitution of our being can be transmitted to others—which means that what is at all communicable is the result of intellection or conceptualization. We humans all aspire to perfect communication, but every form of communication implies some kind of medium. And as soon as we appeal to a medium the original experience is lost or at least loses its personal value. The retention of this value, which makes up the reality or vitality or intimacy of the experience, is possible only where the recipient himself has the same experience. In fact, whatever communication at all effective takes place only between minds that share the same experience. Love is possible only among those who already have the sense for romance. *Satori* is not a feeling, but it has the quality of incommunicableness in the sense that where there is no mentality there is no understanding. Sir Charles is right when he goes on to say: "One gathers that *satori* is not a mystery or secret or anything intellectual which can be imparted. It is a new view of life and of the universe which must be felt."*

What has the *satori*-awakening to do with the arts?

* *Japanese Buddhism,* p. 401.

Let us see what further Sir Charles Eliot has to say on this subject:

When a sect boldly states that its doctrine must be felt and not read and that every attempt to state it in speech or writing must be *ipso facto* a failure, the expositor need say no more. Yet the rash pen longs to formulate the ineffable and is apt to suggest that the mysteries which cannot be expressed in words are really non-existent and that the literary history of Zen, though copious, is not a heap of philosophic jewels buried in a little dust but a farrago of anecdotes reporting grotesque and irrelevant sayings and still more grotesque and often brutal actions. I confess that I am not quite in sympathy with the Zen view of things, and that is why I wish to emphasize the great practical achievements of the sect and to point out that a creed which has produced such remarkable results must be based on something more than eccentricity.*

As long as one tries to see Zen through what the author of *Japanese Buddhism* is tempted to call its "grotesque" or "irrelevant" or "eccentric" sayings and its "brutal" actions, one can never get into the secrets of its "great practical achievements." For Zen is to be located not where these apparently "grotesque" expressions are given, but at the source-experience out of which everything that may shock some of the intellectually-disposed observers would come. The source is the *satori*-awakening. The expressions in

---

* *Ibid.*, p. 399.

words or in actions are derivatives and we are not to strive to get into the source by means of these superficialities. To understand Zen and its remarkable achievements we must look within ourselves and tap the fountainhead itself, that is, we must have a *satori*-experience ourselves.

The Oriental artists in explaining their works make frequent references to such philosophical terms as "Heaven" (*ten, t'ien*), "spirit" (*rei, ling*), "superhuman" (*shin, shên*), "energy" (*ki, ch'i*), "sincerity or integrity" (*makoto, chêng*), "truth" (*shin, chên*), "reason" (*ri, li*), "the nature" (*sei, hsing*), etc. One Japanese critic of art writes: "Is it done by Heaven (*t'ien*)? Or is it man's doing? My doing is what Heaven makes me do. My movements are Heaven's. When a man has no selfish motivation and keeps his mind entirely empty, it becomes one with Heaven. Let him do his utmost in all sincerity, and he will be able to reach his nature (*hsing*). Nature and spirit (*ling*), human and superhuman, becoming one, great works of art are created."*

The opening to what the author here calls "Heaven" (*t'ien*) is attained by means of the *satori*-awakening. While the awakening in itself is not creative, it breaks into a treasure-house behind the consciousness where all sorts of potentialities have been kept in imprisonment. The *satori*

---

* A free rendering from Taketsu-sho Saiji's *Doku Bokkon*, (a work on painting and calligraphy), 1884, fas. 3, 9b.

It is interesting to note what Jacques Maritain writes in his book on art, *Creative Intuition in Art and Poetry* (Meridian Edition, p. 107): "The creative self is both revealing itself and sacrificing itself, because it is *given*; it is drawn out of itself in that sort of ecstasy which is creation, it dies to itself in order to live in the work (how humbly and defenselessly)."

would now release them and give them chances for free play. This is where "Heaven" revealing itself directs the human hand with the brush to work on paper or canvas. From the human point of view it is Emptiness or the spirit of Emptiness which has never been obscured. When this source is not given adequate appreciation, we are apt to take up its outward expressions only and regard them as ultimate. It is true that where there are no expressions there is no question of going beyond them. But we must remember that there are ways and ways of probing the expressions so called. When we think we have exhausted all the means to study them, somebody else comes in and takes up the same old material and discovers what his predecessors failed to see. The world in which we live is an old world, yet we have not exhausted its contents, not only in larger things but in smaller things, too. In fact, we can never reach the end of our researches as long as we limit ourselves to the fields of sense and intellect. This is in the very nature of the human constitution. But, strangely enough, as soon as we quit this realm known as objectivity and turn inward and go on in this direction with resolution and persistency we finally come to a gate known as "the gate of all wonders." We enter through it and find ourselves in the field of Emptiness where we have our being firmly rooted.

Jacques Maritain says, "This essential disinterestedness of the poetic art means that egoism is the natural enemy of poetic activity."* When this egoism which is the natural

---

* *Ibid.*

enemy, not only of poetic activity but of every human activity that is worthy to be called truly human, is removed we have what Oriental philosophy terms "Emptiness" or "Heaven" or "super-personal energy" (*ch'i*) *, and it is by means of this that everything of creative art is accomplished. The *satori*-awakening is no other than "creative intuition," which in terms of Buddhism is *prajñā*-intuition. Zen discipline aims at our attaining this.

---

* *Ch'i* is a very difficult term to translate into English. It is a kind of universal creative energy or spirit which fills "heaven and earth," and from which all beings are formed. "Mind" (*hsin*) is personal and conscious whereas "Energy" (*ch'i*) is super-personal and belongs in the realm of what I call the cosmic unconscious.

V

HEAVEN, NATURE, EMPTINESS

Chuang-tzu, one of the great Taoist philosophers, makes frequent references in his writings to "the perfect man as living when time has not yet come to existence," "abiding with the reason of endlessness," "attaining the formlessness of things," "in unison with Heaven." Further, "the perfect man," says Chuang-tzu, "holds his nature in complete unity, nourishes his energy (*ch'i*) in full vigor, keeps all his activity in harmony, and thereby is in communion with the creator of things. He is thus perfect in guarding his Heaven and he preserves his spirit in absolute integrity so as not to allow any external object to disturb it."

This state of mind of the perfect man is not to be identified with a state of mere concentration, for it is the outcome of one's mind going deeper and being in touch with the source or "ancestor" of all things. A drunken man sometimes attains to this state of mind when he is oblivious of all external things. But his case has nothing to do with his spiritual integrity or with the *satori*-awakening or a deeper insight into the formlessness of things. Chuang-tzu describes his case in the following way:

> When a drunken man falls from the carriage, he may get hurt but will not die. His bones and joints are just the same as those of other people, but the injury he sustains is different. This is due to his spirit

(*shên*) being integrated. While riding he is not conscious of it. Life and death, fear and anxiety, do not enter into his breast. Therefore, when he encounters events he is not frightened by them. If such a spiritual integration is possible from drinking, how much more when the integration is gained from Heaven! The wise man abides in Heaven, therefore nothing will ever hurt him.

A revengeful man would not try to break the sword [which injured him]; nor would one who is easily offended blame the flying tile [which accidentally hit him]. [Neither the sword nor the tile has any human wilfulness; they are not to be blamed for whatever injury they have given the man.] If we were thus free [from a self-assertive malice] the whole world would be at peace, and there would be no disorderly fightings, no punitive slaughterings. All this comes from observing the way [of Heaven], that is, from revealing heavenly Heaven instead of revealing humanly Heaven. To those who reveal Heavenliness virtues come, but to those who reveal humanliness woes come. Do not suppress Heaven in us, do not neglect human affairs, and then we will be nearer to what is true.

Li Po (701–62), the great poet of the T'ang dynasty, is said to have drunk heavily when he wanted to produce fine poetical compositions. He was not the only one who wished for an intoxicating substance. The reason we crave for it is probably due to our unconscious desire to be freed from all kinds of inhibitions which we moderns go on creating all around us. When the obstructions are removed, the unconscious is freer to function, and artists feel at ease to display whatever "heavenliness" they have within them.*

This is the case with the artists who depend on external agents such as canvas and paints, or all kinds of sound-producing instruments, or marble, or metal, or blocks, or wood. With "the perfect man," however, there is no need for these things, he is at home in his own body, which is always ready to turn into the most efficient instrument for the execution of Heaven that is hidden within himself. Nature has given every one of us a form which he can shape in any way he likes, beautiful or ugly, lovable or hateful, attractive or repulsive. It was Lincoln, I understand, who said that after forty years a man's face is one which he has made himself. This is a most significant saying, showing how keen an observer of humanity Lincoln was. One's facial expressions betray everything that goes on in the soul. The

---

* One of Li Po's poems, entitled "Waking from Drunkenness on a Spring Day," reads as follows:

'Life in the world is but a big dream;
I will not spoil it by any labour or care.'
So saying, I was drunk all day,
Lying helpless at the porch in front of my door.
When I woke up I looked into the garden court;
A single bird was singing amid the flowers.
I asked myself, what season is this?
Restless the oriole chatters in the spring breeze.
Moved by its song I soon began to sigh
And, as wine was there, I filled my own cup.
Noisily singing I waited for the moon to rise;
When my song was over, all my sense had gone.
                    (Arthur Waley's translation)

soul looks through the eyes, and those who know read it. In fact, the soul expresses itself not only through the eyes, or the facial muscles, but by the entire body and its every movement. The body implements the soul and in this respect we are all artists. The soul's creations are transferred onto the body, and in proportion to the genuineness of the soul's work the body transparently reflects this quality. The body mirrors the purity of the soul. To use Chuang-tzu's terms, when the heavenliness of Heaven attains its original integrity or sincerity one is a "perfect man" who has no fears whatever, walking over and through the ten thousand things.

To continue with Chuang-tzu, as he has so much of Zen, the heavenliness of Heaven consists in making the horse or the ox go four-legged, while it is humanliness to control the horse with a halter or to put a string through the bull's nose. Strictly speaking, there is no humanliness because it too is of Heaven; man did not get what he is from anywhere else. If he happens to go against Heaven it is really Heaven going against itself. Christians may say, "God is revolting against himself," or "He is destroying His work." But in spite of this logicalness there is something in man that makes him feel that he is not doing everything in the way Heaven wants him to do. And it is thus that he talks so much about the duality of Heaven and man, of heavenliness and humanness, of divinity and man's sinfulness, and so on. Let us, however, go on here with our actual feelings instead of trying to probe into the reason of all this and discussing the matter philosophically. That is to say, we are human and quite frequently act against Heaven. Instead of being one with Heaven, we abuse our intellect and contrive all kinds of things to destroy Heaven which is in us and which really keeps us in good order not only physically but spiritually. So Chuang-tzu as well as Zen advises us to practice "non-action" or "no-mind-ness" or "no-thought-ness." Chuang-tzu thus makes the Yellow Emperor say: "By having no thoughts, no contrivances, one knows what Tao is; by having no abode, no clothing, one is at peace with Tao; by having nothing to depend upon, no way (*tao*) for guidance, one has Tao."

This point is well illustrated by the story of a fighting cock.

Chi Hsing-tzu was training a fighting cock for the prince. When ten days passed, the prince asked, "Is it ready for fighting?" Chi answered, "Not yet, sir, he is still vain and full of fighting spirit." Another ten days passed and the prince asked again, "Not ready yet?" Chi answered, "He listens to the crow of another cock and pursues its shadow." After another ten days the same question was asked, and Chi said, "No, sir, not yet. He is still excitable and exuberant with spirit." When ten more days elapsed, the prince made another inquiry. Chi said, "He is almost ready. Though another cock crows, he remains unmoved. When he is looked at, he resembles one made of wood. His virtue is perfect. No cocks are his match, they will hastily run away from him."

To train a fighting cock like one made of wood is the Taoist way, which is reflected in the Zen teaching of purpose-lessness, of not leaving any track or footsteps, of a circle whose circumference is infinite with a center everywhere, of planting flowers on the rock, of the donkey looking down into the well. All these dicta come, psychologically speaking, from the state of selflessness, and, metaphysically, from the notion of Emptiness. Chuang-tzu's "Heaven," or non-action, corresponds to this, and "Nature" symbolizes it. Man's humanliness or his crafty intelligence tries to tamper with Nature or Heaven, and when he has succeeded in making the atomic bomb he imagines he has conquered or harnessed Nature to his service. He, however, is at a loss just at this present moment as to how to avoid annihilating the whole of humanity, including all living beings on this planet. It is the most presumptuous and most absurd idea of ours to think that we are the master of all existences. And when we face death, we are given up to fears and know not what to do with the nothingness which we think comes after death or after general slaughtering. Where is our boasted mastership? What about "the awful finality of death?" As long as we are slaves of the power-idea and turn human craftiness into its subservient instrument, we must never think of bringing peace on earth, for we are sure to be involved somehow in one or another sort of imbroglio, political, economic, or otherwise. Chuang-tzu gives another illustration to convince us of the practical advantages of the Emptiness theory.

Suppose a man is crossing a stream in a boat. He sees another boat about to collide with his. He cautions it about the approaching danger. Not hearing any response he shouts. Still no answer. He gets angry this time and uses bad language. But when he finally discovers that the boat in question has no passenger in it, being empty, he realizes his stupidity or overhastiness. This is because in the first case he thought there was a man in the boat, which angered him, whereas in the second case he found out the boat was devoid of any person. So it is with us. If we go along in life with nothing in mind, who can harm us?

The Buddhist idea of Emptiness is very liable to be misunderstood, as we are ordinarily bound up with things of relativity and regard Emptiness as one of these. But the Buddhist idea as well as the Taoists' is metaphysical and has a decidedly positive connotation. Emptiness is not sheer nothingness. This is to be remembered especially when we peruse Zen texts. They resort to the use of negative terms because as soon as we have something to assert this is apt to be taken in its relative sense. When the master producing the staff demands that we say something about it, he will reject any statement we may make of it. Seeing that our logical or linguistic resources are exhausted he will come down from the pulpit and walk away with his staff supporting him. Emptiness walks with the staff as well as with the master, because he is master of things and not one of them. If he were a thing, his Emptiness would no more be with him. As Chuang-tzu says, "The Perfect Man treats things as things and is not thinged by things." He roams in the Field of Emptiness with the Ancestor of the ten thousand things.

Therefore Tokusan (Tê-shan, 782–865) gave the following sermon: "I am not going to have you ask me any question this evening. If you do, I will give you thirty blows of my stick." A monk came forward and began to bow before the master. The master did not lose any time in striking him. The monk, however, protested, "When I have not yet asked you any question, why do you strike me, O Master?" The master said, "Where do you come from?" The monk answered, "From Korea." The master declared. "Even before you boarded the boat, you deserved thirty blows of mine!"

When this behavior on the part of Tokusan is understood, we can say that this man understands what Zen is and what the *satori*-awakening is. And also we can concede that he has come to the heavenliness of Heaven which is in man, and that he now understands the significance of the empty boat with no boatman in it, of the fighting cock standing like one made of wood that has no fighting spirit. Chinese critics of art talk about "the vital movement of spiritual rhythm"* in the lines of a fine work of art. The spiritual rhythm, so called, is attained only when the artist forgets that it is he who is handling the brush.

---

* J. *shin-in seidō*; C. *shên-yün shêng-tung.*

VI

THE TRAINING IN ZEN

As Zen aims at attaining enlightenment or experiencing *satori*-awakening, it has a number of training schools organized for the purpose. They are called "Semmon Dōjō" or simply "Sōdō" or "Zendō." The monks and laymen who wish to study Zen come here and go through several years of hard training. Strictly speaking, Zen is no more, no less than our daily life, and there is nothing to teach specifically designated as Zen. But as Zen differentiated itself as such and has a long history behind it, it has developed its own method of training students. For one thing it emphasizes the significance of manual labor. While it practices so-called meditation known as *zazen,* it keeps the monks otherwise fully occupied with all kinds of work: cleaning, sweeping, washing, cooking, farming, etc. The monastery grounds are generally kept in good order; for this the monks are well known. They also have to go out for a round of begging for rice on certain days each month. Their discipline is almost military as far as its precision is concerned, but it goes without saying that it is thoroughly imbued with the spirit of compassion and cooperation.

The importance of manual labor was fully recognized in the earliest history of Zen, and not only the monks but the master shared in the general work of the monastery. In Zen there is no mind apart from the body and no body apart from the mind, they are one. Conceptualization is apt to emphasize the mind in a most undesirably unbalanced way. Therefore, in the midst of work the master would frequently take hold of a monk and ask him, "What is it that you are carrying along?" or "I hear your voice but where is your being?"

The Japanese master of swordplay sometimes uses the Zen method of training. When a disciple came to a master to be disciplined in the art of swordplay, the master, who was in retirement in his mountain hut, agreed to undertake the task. The pupil was made to help him gather kindlings, draw water from the nearby spring, split wood to make fire, cook rice, sweep the rooms and the garden, and generally look after his household affairs. There was no regular or technical teaching in the art. After some time the young man became dissatisfied, for he had not come to work as servant to the old gentleman, but to learn the art of swordsmanship. So one day he approached the master and asked to be taught. The master agreed.

The result was that the young man could not do any piece of work with any feeling of safety. For when he began to cook rice early in the morning, the master would appear and strike him from behind with a stick. When he was in the midst of his sweeping, he would be feeling the same blow from somewhere, from an unknown direction. He had no peace of mind, he had to be always on the *qui vive*. Some years passed before he could successfully dodge the blow from whatever source it might come. But the master was not quite satisfied with him yet.

One day the master was found cooking his own vegetables

over an open fire. The pupil took it into his head to avail himself of this opportunity. Taking up his big stick, he let it fall over the head of the master, who was then stooping over the cooking pan to stir its contents. But the pupil's stick was caught by the master with the cover of the pan. This opened the pupil's mind to the secrets of the art, which had hitherto been kept away from him and to which he had yet been a stranger. He then for the first time really appreciated the unparalleled kindness of the master.

In this there is something of the Zen method of training, which consists in personally experiencing the truth, whatever this may be, and not appealing to intellection or systematic theorization. The latter busies itself with the details of technique, and is consequently superficial and never leads to the central fact of the matter. Theorization may be all very well when building factories, constructing fortresses, manufacturing industrial goods or murderous instruments of various kinds, but not with creating objects of art, or mastering arts which are direct expressions of the human soul, or acquiring the art of living a life true to itself. Anything, in fact, which has to do with creation in its genuine sense is really "untransmittable," that is, beyond the ken of discursive understanding. Hence Zen's motto, "No reliance on words."

In this respect Zen is opposed to everything that goes by the name of science or scientific. Zen is personal, while science is impersonal. What is impersonal is abstract and does not take notice of individual experiences. What is personal belongs altogether to the individual and has no signification without the backing of his own experience.

Science means systematization, and Zen is just its reverse. Words are needed in science and philosophy, but they are a hindrance in Zen. Why? Because words are representations and not realities, and realities are what is most highly valued in Zen. If words are needed in Zen, they are of the same value as coins in trading. We cannot wear coins to keep the cold away, we cannot eat coins to quench thirst or appease hunger. Coins are to be turned into real food, real wool, and real water when they are of real value to life. We are constantly forgetting this homely truth, and never cease hoarding money. In a similar manner we memorize words and play with concepts and think we are wise. "Wise" indeed we are, but this kind of wisdom never avails when dealing with the realities of life. If it did is it not high time we had a millenium by now?

Roughly speaking, there are three kinds of knowledge. The first is such as we gain from reading or hearsay, which we memorize and usually hold as an important possession; the bulk of knowledge, so called, is of this kind. We cannot walk all over the earth and personally survey it, and therefore for the knowledge of the world we depend upon a map which has been prepared for us by others. The second kind of knowledge is what is ordinarily known as scientific. It is the result of observation and experiment, analysis and speculation. It has a firmer foundation than the former, for here is something personal and experienced to a certain extent. The third kind of knowledge is the one attained by an intuitive mode of understanding. According to those who hold to the second form of knowledge, the intuitive kind is regarded as having no solid foundation in fact and, therefore, as not absolutely reliable. But as a matter of fact scientific knowledge, so called, is not at all exhaustive and for that reason awaits further corrections, for it is confined to a sphere of its own limitation. When an emergency, especially of a personal nature, arises, science and logic may have no time to make use of their store of knowledge and calculation, nor may memorized knowledge be available, for then the mind may fail to recall all it has accumulated in the past. Intuitive knowledge, on the other hand, forms the basis of all kinds of faith, especially religious, and most efficiently and successfully rises up to meet crises.

Concepts are needed for general use and also for practical utilization. But as long as they are general and meant for public purposes they are not private, they do not belong to you in any specific sense. When you want to use them they may not be ready for you. They serve you only when they grow out of yourself, that is, when they are your exclusive possession. You cannot transmit the experience to others, unless they, too, have it growing out of their inner being for themselves. The following story, told by Goso Hōyen (Fa-yen, died 1104), of the Sung dynasty, will help us greatly in our understanding of the Zen method and Zen spirit which have been described as being against teaching based on intellect, logic, and verbalism:

> If people ask me what Zen is like, I will say that it is like learning the art of burglary. The son of a burglar saw his father growing older and thought, 'If he is unable to carry out his profession, who will be the breadwinner of this family except myself? I must learn the trade.' He intimated this to his father, who approved of it. One

night the father took the sōn to a big house, broke through the fence, entered the house, and, opening one of the large chests, told the son to go in and pick out the clothing. As soon as he got into it, the lid was dropped and the lock securely applied. The father now went out to the courtyard, and loudly knocking at the door woke up the whole family. Then he himself quietly slipped away through the former hole in the fence. The people of the house got excited and lighted candles, but found that the burglar had already gone. The son, who had remained all the time in the chest securely confined, thought of his cruel father. He was greatly mortified, when a fine idea flashed upon him. He made a noise which sounded like the gnawing of a rat. The family told the maid to take a candle and examine the chest. When the lid was unlocked, out came the prisoner, who blew out the light, pushed away the maid, and fled. The people ran after him. Noticing a well by the road, he picked up a large stone and threw it into the water. Trying to find the burglar drowning himself in the dark hole, the pursuers all gathered around the well. In the meantime he was safely back in his father's house. He blamed his father very much for his narrow escape. Said the father, 'Be not offended, my son. Just tell me how you got off.' When the son had told him all about his adventures, the father remarked, 'There you are, you have learned the art.'

This radical method of teaching the art of burglary aptly illustrates the methodology of Zen. When a disciple asks his master to teach Zen to him, the latter may slap his face and exclaim, "What a good-for-nothing fellow you are!"

When one approaches the master with the question, "I have a doubt about the truth which is said to liberate us from the bondage of the passions," or with some such question, the master may take him before the entire congregation of monks and declare, "Look, O monks, here is one who cherishes a doubt!" He may then push the poor monk away from his presence, while he himself nonchalantly retires to his own quarters. It appears as if doubting were criminal, or at least something one ought never to cherish where all is open for one's free and unobstructed inspection. If the master is asked whether he understands Buddhism, he will say, "No, I do not." Further asked, "Who understands Buddhism, then?" he will point at the pillar just outside his study.

When the Zen master makes a show of the logician, he goes altogether contrary to the usual method of reasoning and valuation. Not only in this case "Fair is foul and foul is fair," but "You are I and I am you." Facts, so called, are ignored, values become topsy-turvy. Perhaps until the world is turned upside down, or until, as Buddhists would say, the world all burns up at the end of the present kalpa, we may not be able to understand what Zen is.

Some of you may protest and exclaim, "What nonsense you've been talking about! If we have to wait for such a long period and for such a catastrophe to understand Zen, why have you troubled yourself at all to write this book?" My answer is, "You do not have to wait really so long. Zen knows no time and therefore there is to Zen no beginning of the world, no ending of the world. This very moment you are talking to me is the end of the world and at the same time the beginning of the world. When the present moment is grasped everything will be all clear to you."

"How then do we grasp the Eternal Now?" you may ask.

"Listen! Don't you hear an airplane whirling over our heads?"

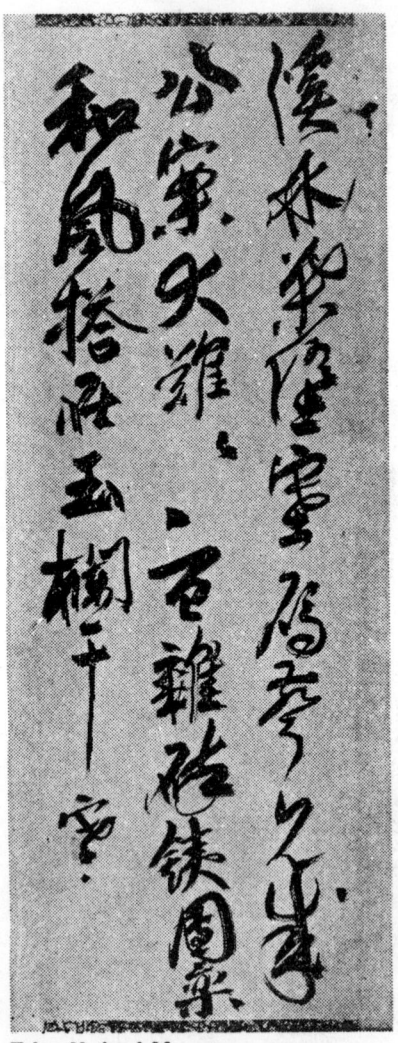

Tokyo National Museum

A Chinese poem, portraying the serene and quiet state of the Zen mind, composed and written by Daitō Kokushi in *sumi* ink on paper. Many of the poems and letters written by Zen priests of deep spiritual attainments are works of art.

(Owned by Mr. Takayuki Masaki.)

PART II

JAPANESE BUDDHISM

"Śākyamuni Preaching the Dharma." (Done in embroidery in the 6th or 7th century. Owned by the National Commission for the Protection of Cultural Properties.)

Tokyo National Museum

A section of "Five Hundred Rakan." (Painted in color on silk in the 5th century. Treasure of Tōfukuji Temple, Kyoto City.)

Fugen, the Bodhisattva of Charity and Prolongation of Life. (Painted in color on silk in the 12th century. Owned by the Tokyo National Museum.)

Tokyo National Museum

Monju, the Bodhisattva of Wisdom. (Painted in color on silk in the 13th or 14th century. Treasure of Daigoji Temple, Kyoto City.)

I

THE TWO MAIN SCHOOLS OF BUDDHISM

Buddhism is divisible into two main schools: Hinayana or "smaller vehicle," also known as the Theravada school, and Mahayana or "greater vehicle." Japanese Buddhism belongs to the latter. Some of the major differences between the Hinayana and the Mahayana are:

(1) Historically, the Hinayana or the Theravada is older than the Mahayana, though this does not mean that the former represents more faithfully the teaching of the founder. On the contrary, Mahayana claims that Hinayana more or less failed to develop the most important aspects of the original teaching and is inclined to uphold a formal and literal and scholastic interpretation of it. The result was the fossilization of the spirit of Buddha. The Mahayana was not at all satisfied with this. It began to assert itself within a hundred years after the passing of Buddha, until its movement became strong enough in the first century before Christ to call itself "the Mahayana school" in contradistinction to the earlier one, which the later Buddhists designated as "the Hinayana." By this they meant that their teaching was more far-reaching and all-embracing than that of their older fellow-believers.

(2) The ideal person of the Hinayana teaching is called Arhat, or Rakan in Japanese. He is one who has attained

the state of enlightenment by his moral efforts through the eons. He remains contented with this and has no special desire to extend the merit of enlightenment to his fellow-beings. He thinks that each individual has to look after his own salvation, and that all that one can do for others is to persuade or exhort, beyond which nothing can be done. The Arhat is a rigid upholder of spiritual individualism. Unless a man works for his own enlightenment and emancipation, he cannot reach the other shore of *saṃsāra* (birth-and-death); others, however sympathetic, cannot help him cross the stream. The Arhat is, therefore, also a strong advocate of intellectualism.

The Mahayanists did not think that this austere individualism was in strict accord with the spirit of Buddha. It is true that he attained his enlightenment after going through many a rebirth, every one of which was vigorously devoted to the exercise of the six virtues of perfection (called *pāramitā*); but his enlightenment was not for his individual benefit only; it was meant for all sentient beings. Unless the latter, too, share in it in some way, it has no significance for the world. Whatever merit there is in it ought to be universally spread among all beings. This is the way we as human beings feel towards our fellow-beings. In the Mahayana, therefore, love all-inclusive and all-penetrating comes out, in great contrast to the Hinayanists' unequivocal tendency towards intellectual and moral isolationism.

The Bodhisattva (or Bosatsu in Japanese) is the ideal personage of the Mahayana. He starts his religious career from his "never-to-be-extinguished" desire to save all his fellow-beings, including everything that exists, and for this object he will work to the end of his life, even going through many rebirths if that is necessary.

(3) The Hinayanists are adherents of ascetic rigorism, for they maintain that unless a person is able to practice this kind of life there is no hope for him to achieve the final end of the Buddhist life, which is a complete subjugation of all passions and desires, and this subjugation or rather extinction is impossible outside the monastic life of the Sangha Brotherhood. Those who could not leave their family life and devote themselves to the austerities of the spiritual life were doomed to recurring births full of pain and misery. But if they followed the teaching of Buddha and joined his Brotherhood and paid due reverence in various practical ways to the ascetic monks, they might be born in a more favorable state in their next lives, so that they could leave home and join the Buddhist Brotherhood. This was their only hope for final emancipation.

The Mahayanists naturally revolted against this idea of salvation, which is really for the *élite*. If a religion means, they thought, to benefit us spiritually, this benefit must have a universal character. Buddha's idea was to save all beings by having them believe in the truth which was discovered by him and which is also discoverable by all who would follow him. Ultimate enlightenment does not consist in extinguishing the passions and desires shared by all sentient beings; rather, it detaches such passions and desires from their selfish origin and encumbrances, so that they can be made available for the establishment of a universal brotherhood. Householders ought to be able to attain enlightenment just as well as homeless ones, i.e., monks, if only they have an intuitive understanding of the truth. The Mahayanists with this view compiled many scriptures.

(4) As the Hinayanists were strict interpreters of the rules of morality, called Vinaya (*kairitsu* in Japanese), they failed to spread their teaching to other countries where the climate was not adapted to the maintenance of their way of living. Buddhism did not begin to propagate itself beyond the borders of its birth-land until the rise of the Mahayana— I mean to the northern countries where a more rigorous climate, necessitating modifications in the life of the Buddhist monk, prevailed. This naturally meant changes in the doctrinal interpretation of so-called original or primitive Buddhism. A liberal spirit was to be emphasized at the expense of formalism, that is, the conservative upholding of the letter of the Vinaya rules had to go. Thus, the Mahayana came to be identified with the spirit of progress, freedom, and liberalism generally. It was as one of the manifestations of this spirit on the part of the Mahayanists that Buddha now came to assume a double aspect, historical and metaphysical or spiritual. To the Mahayanists, Buddha is not only a being naturally and historically limited, but one who goes beyond all forms of causal determination, and who, therefore, is able to assume any form of existence according to the conditions. The Mahayanists hold this point as one of the strongest positions in their system of philosophy.

(5) The Mahayana idea of "skilful means" (*hōben* in Japanese and *upāya* in Sanskrit), according to which supreme Buddhahood incarnates itself in a variety of forms in order to save all beings from ignorance and misery, has produced a number of Buddhas and Bodhisattvas and even

"supernatural beings" in the Buddhist scheme of cosmology. This is the reason why the Mahayana is sometimes regarded as polytheistic. The Mahayanist reasoning, however, is that salvation is to be achieved in conformity with the mentality of beings, that is, with their intellectual capacity to grasp the truth. What a child wants is a mechanical toy and not a real engine whose handling demands a great deal of technical knowledge. As long as our mental and spiritual endowments are severally graded—in fact, subject to infinite gradation—the doctrine of "skilful means" which distinguishes the Mahayana from the Hinayana must be said to be in agreement with the facts of human experience. For this reason the Buddhist figures, which are enshrined in the Mahayana temples of the Far East, are variously formed. They are really symbolical representations of the virtues and powers of the One Buddha.

(6) The Mahayanists are more broad-minded and liberal-spirited than their elder brothers, the Hinayanists, not only in their practical way of living but also in their philosophy and conception of the world generally. In this, however, they are sometimes apt to go too far, as they allow too much latitude to the understanding of the teaching of Buddha. Their latitudinarianism thus occasionally proves too antinomian. Rigidity and liberality, Hinayana and Mahayana, are to be so set against each other as to ensure for Buddhism the best result of each tendency, especially in practical matters of life.

II

THE DEVELOPMENT OF
JAPANESE BUDDHISM

Japanese Buddhism belongs to the Mahayana school, and as it has developed in this country for more than a thousand years entirely independently of Hinayana influence, it presents in various ways quite a different form of Buddhism from that persisting in Ceylon, Thailand, and Burma.

(1) Buddhism was officially introduced to Japan from Chōsen (Korea) in 552 A.D., when the King of Kudara presented to the Emperor Kimmei (reigning 539–572) a bronze image of Śākyamuni together with sūtras and religious objects. But it is possible that some of the immigrants from the Asiatic continent who had settled prior to the above date were Buddhists, and that their religion was making quiet progress among the people. The Emperor Kimmei was not quite sure as to what kind of reception he would accord the new faith, for his court officials were divided into two factions. The struggle for supremacy went on for some time, but the Buddhist party finally won the day.

About fifty years after the official introduction, Prince Shōtoku Taishi (574–622), whose name is never to be forgotten in the history of Japanese Buddhism and culture, became regent to the Empress Suiko (reigning 592–628), his aunt, and it was owing to his patronage and devotion that Buddhism struck firm root on Japanese soil. He built many

Portrait of Prince Shōtoku Taishi. (Painted in color on silk in the 13th century. Treasure of Ninnaji Temple, Kyoto City.)

Asukaen

84

Tatsuzo Satō

Horyūji Temple, Nara Prefecture. The two-storied building on the right of the pagoda is the Main Hall. The Lecture Hall is seen in the background.

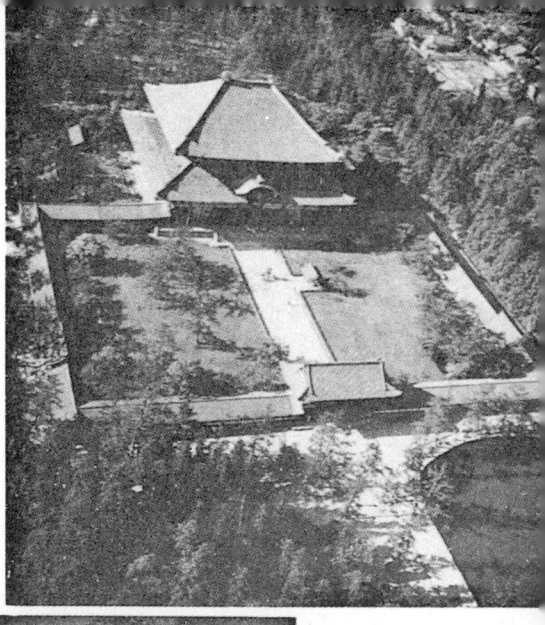

The Great Buddha of the Tōdaiji Temple in Nara City, and an aerial view of the Buddha Hall.

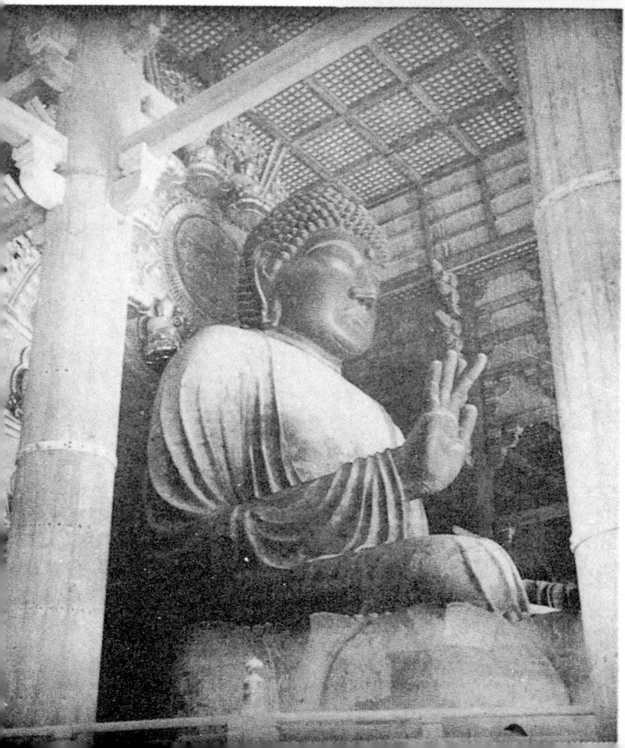

Japan Travel Bureau

Portrait of Dengyō Daishi. (Painted in color on silk in the 12th
century. Treasure of Ichijoji Temple, Hyogo Prefecture.)

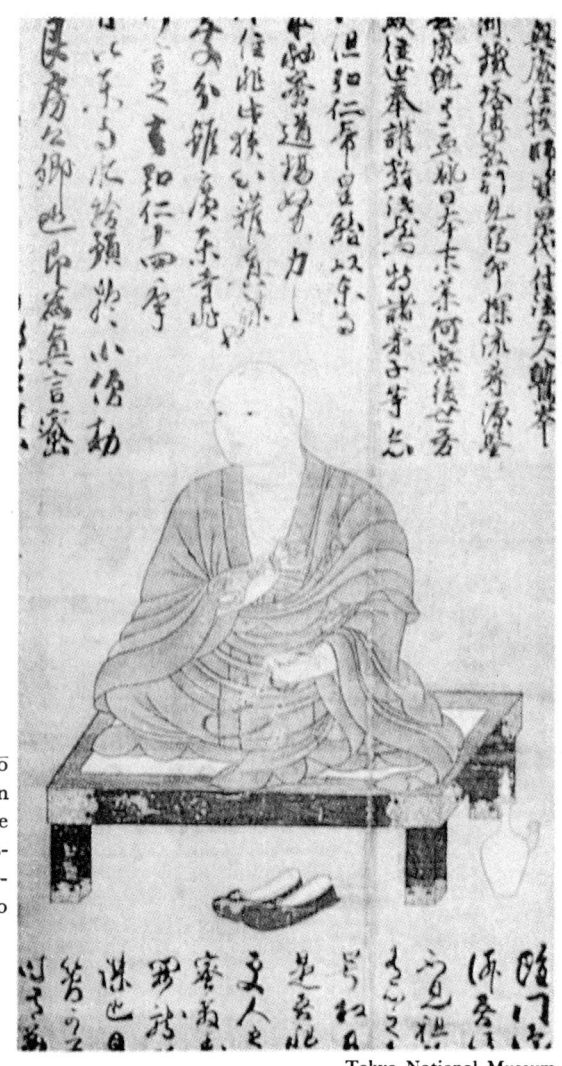

Portrait of Kōbō Daishi. (Painted in color on silk in the 14th century. Treasure of Kyō-ō-goko-kuji Temple, Kyoto City.)

Tokyo National Museum

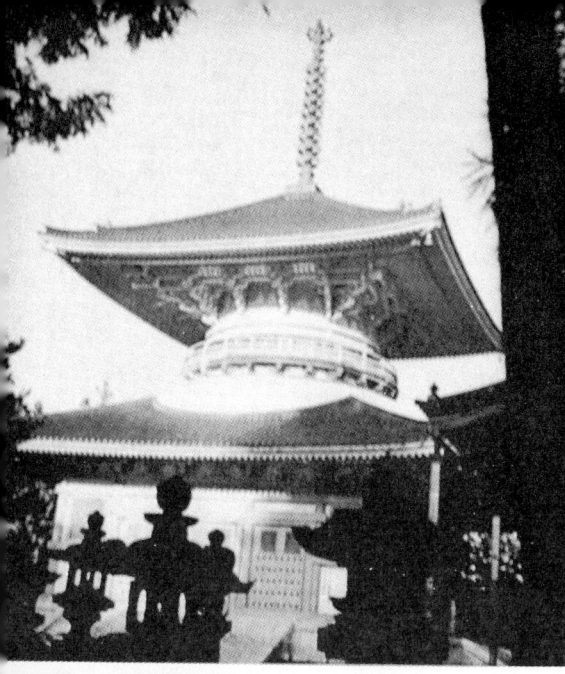

Kompon Daitō (Great Central Pagoda) of the Kongōbuji Temple, founded by Kōbo Daishi, on Mt. Kōya, Wakayama Prefecture.

Japan Travel Bureau

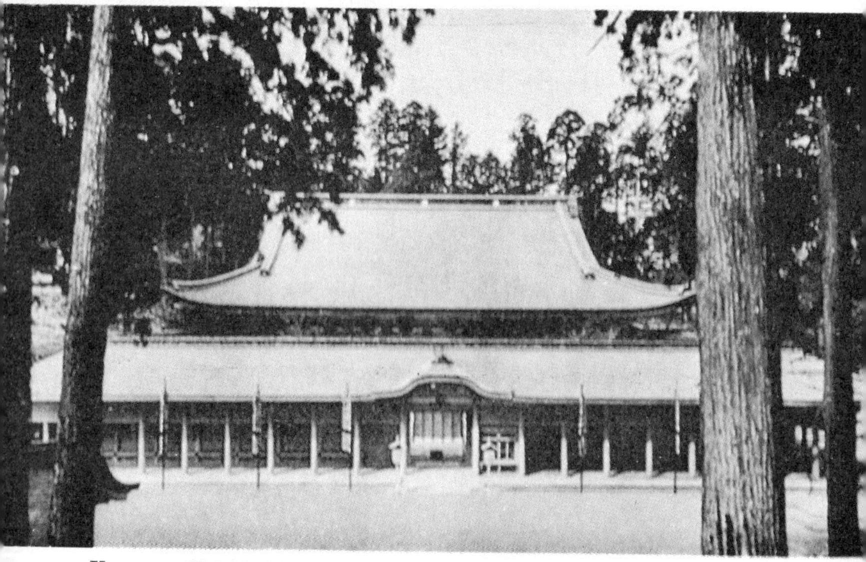

Kompon Chūdō (Great Central Hall) of the Enryakuji Temple, founded by Dengyō Daishi, on Mt. Hiei, Ōtsu City.

fine temples in Nara and vicinity, among which was Hōryūji, still in existence. He was a great scholar, and wrote commentaries on the three important Buddhist Sūtras: the *Puṇḍarīka* (*Hokekyō* in Japanese), *Śrīmālā* (*Shōmangyō*), and *Vimalakīrti* (*Yuimakyō*). In those days Buddhism meant progress and indeed everything that was of social and cultural value.

(2) Buddhism of the Nara and earlier periods (593–784) was not divided into definite sects as we now know them, but we can distinguish the following six schools that flourished in Nara: the *Abhidharmakośa* (Kusha in Japanese), *Satyasiddhi* (Jōjitsu), *Vinaya* (Ritsu), *Yogācāra* (Hossō), *Mādhyamika* (Sanron), and *Avatamsaka* or *Gandhavyūha* (Kegon). Teachers belonging to these schools wrote many commentaries on the sūtras. It is wonderful to note that they were all products of learned scholarship, showing how eagerly those Japanese Buddhists took up the study of Buddhism, which was to them a new philosophy, a new science, a new religion, a new culture, and an inexhaustible mine of artistic impulses and subjects.

The building of many temples and monasteries, the maintenance of monks and nuns, the erection of the gigantic bronze image of Vairocana (Daibutsu, finished in 749)—all these expenses were defrayed from the government exchequer. We may wonder how the government came to engage in such undertakings. The truth is, however, that we ought not to judge the religion in a modern light; for in those days the Buddhist temples were schools, hospitals, dispensaries, orphanages, refuges for old age; and the monks were schoolmasters, nurses, doctors, engineers, keepers of free lodges, cultivators of land, explorers of the wildernesses, etc. When the community was still in a primitive stage of evolution, the Buddhists were leaders in every sense, and the government naturally encouraged their activities.

We at this late date cannot fully realize what the building of the Tōdaiji and the casting of the gigantic bronze statue of Buddha Vairocana really meant to the people of the Nara period (710–84). The Tōdaiji, rebuilt after a fire in the twelfth century, is only about two-thirds of the original size, but still it is the largest wooden building under one roof in the world. The Grand Hall originally measured 284 feet long, 166 feet wide, and 156 feet high, while the Great Buddha was about 53 feet high including the double pedestal on which the image was placed. The halo behind it was 114 feet high and 98 feet wide. The amount of metal used is said to have been over one million pounds. All these works must have involved all the labor and money the Emperor and his advisers could command in those early days. Modern critics may have their views about these undertakings, but there is no doubt they were a great stimulus morally, financially, culturally, and even physically to the national aspirations of the people generally. Nations as well as individuals are occasionally required to take leaps in their lives in order to keep their spiritual energies on the *qui vive*. If this can be done by peaceful means so much the better. Buddhism was the very thing the Japanese people of the Nara period needed for their forward movement in culture and civilization, although this must have meant a great strain on them in every way.

Among other things that have to be mentioned here, there is one which concerns the movement of Buddhist women in the Nara period. The Empress Kōmyō (701–60) and the Empress Kōken (718–70) and the nun Hōkin and others are names to be long remembered by the Japanese as typifying the Buddhist life of love and compassion.

(3) Perhaps the growth of Buddhism was fostered too lavishly or too artificially in the beginning. Although it aided the development of Japanese culture immensely, it became a burden too heavy for the nation of the eighth century to bear, especially financially. And then the favored monks behaved selfishly. The distinction between secular powers and religious attainments began to be blurred. Even in the latter unessentials were brought out more conspicuously at the expense of the essentials. The time came for Buddhism to face about. Nara Buddhism was to be replaced by Heian Buddhism.

The Emperor Kammu (reigned 781–806) moved his capital from Nara to Kyoto towards the end of the eighth century. Against the tradition that had prevailed until then, he left all the old temples in Nara, and established new ones on Mount Hiei and in the south part of the capital. The new leaders represented the Tendai and the Shingon. Dengyō Daishi (767–822) and Kōbō Daishi (774–835), the two greatest leaders of the new régime, stepped forward boldly on the stage.

¶ Every visitor to Kyoto will easily recognize where Mount Hiei stands, for it is the highest of the mountains in the northeast of the city. This was the site selected by Dengyō to establish his Tendai school of Buddhism. He was one of the first Buddhist monks who realized the dangers of the city-life which had been too well enjoyed by his Nara predecessors. He was not only a perfect master of the abstruse philosophy of the T'ien-tai (Tendai), but a profound student of the mystic rites and the *dhyāna* practice. His ambition was to synthesize all the schools of Buddhism that were known in his day. All the new sects of Buddhism that were unfolded later in the Kamakura period (1192–1333) can be traced back to Mount Hiei, the headquarters of Dengyō.

The old schools of Nara were inevitable opponents of the new leaders, not only for sentimental reasons but also for the more important reason of doctrinal differences. For Dengyō belonged to the T'ien-tai school, which upheld the absolutism of the One Vehicle, whereas the old Nara defended the *Yogācāra* doctrine. The issue was concerned with the ultimate character of the teaching of the *Puṇḍarīka* (*Hokekyō*).

Dengyō also wanted to have a special Mahayana ordination platform which was to be independent of Nara. He fought bravely against overwhelming opposition, and his plan was carried out only after his death.

Kōbō Daishi was a contemporary of Dengyō, younger by seven years, and surviving him by twelve years. He belonged to a different type of genius; he was one of the most versatile of men, a profound scholar, an ascetic, an extensive traveler, an artist of the first class, a man of affairs, and a most experienced calligrapher. His chief object of study was the Dainichikyō (*Mahāvairocana Sūtra* in Sanskrit) and the Kongōchōkyō (*Vajraśekhara Sūtra*), the two great text-books of the Shingon sect. While in China he became a disciple of Hui-kuo (Keika Ajari, 746–805) and succeeded him as the eighth patriarch of the Shingon sect.

He opened up Mount Kōya as the headquarters of Shingon mysticism and is regarded by his disciples as still living there in a state of *samādhi* (meditation). He liked to have a monastery in the mountains but did not forget to keep up his connection with the world. The Toji in the south of Kyoto marks his deep footprints in the capital. Dengyō seems to have kept himself too much away from the world and Hiei remains solitary in spite of its nearness to the city. Kōya is (or rather was) an almost inaccessible place compared to Hiei, but how many pilgrims congregate there every year! On the mountain a little town has come into existence.

The Heian period (784–1192) was chiefly taken up by the Shingon and the Tendai, almost overshadowing the old Buddhism of Nara, but at the same time there were signs that they, the Tendai and the Shingon, too, had to give way to the new force which had quietly but steadily been emerging.

(4) The Tendai in its pure form is too philosophical for popular consumption, and it was necessary for it to find a way from its speculative flights back to the hearts of the masses. The way was found in the performing of mystic rites, which, however, properly belong to the Shingon. The Japanese Tendai thus became a mixture of Chinese T'ien-tai metaphysics with the practical ritualism of Shingon; and we can say that the Buddhism of the Heian period was flooded with magical ritualism. To put a stop to evil influences the rite called "Sokusai Hō" was performed; to increase happiness, the "Zōyaku"; to invite good powers, the "Kuso"; to defeat enemies, the "Gofuku"; to pray for the

loving protection of the Buddhas and Bodhisattvas, the "Kyōai"; and to achieve prolongation of life, the "Emmei." All these mystic rites were considered thoroughly effective in bringing about what the devotee desired.

Besides these, there were all kinds of ceremonies performed on different occasions, auspicious or otherwise, at the various chief temples in the land. The performance sometimes lasted a week. As a matter of fact these could be attended only by people of the leisure class, that is, by the nobility of the time. In those days when there were not very many and varied social entertainments, it was natural enough for the nobility to turn some of the Buddhist ceremonials into a sort of refined entertainment to pass their time. That present-day Buddhism still wears an air of aristocracy is no doubt traceable to the traditions of those bygone days.

(5) Aristocratic and ritualistic Buddhism, however, is not of Mahayana Buddhism. When it undergoes such transformations it is high time for it to go back to its original form, that is, democratic and practical and spiritual. While the Shingon was enjoying its heyday of prosperity, there was another movement going on undermining its apparent influence. This was the rise of the Pure Land school, whose principal teaching consists in repeating Buddha's name (Nembutsu) and being born in the country of Amida.

Buddhism was so far confined to the upper classes of society who had enough mentality and leisure to master its abstruse philosophy and its extraordinarily complicated system of rituals. This was inevitable. It first came to Japan through official channels; it aided the Court and those who surrounded it in carrying out their program of national policy. Buddhism became solidly amalgamated with all that was symbolic of power, culture, knowledge, and morality. It was all good as far as it went, but aristocracy is a one-eyed child, it sees the refined surface but lacks solidity and frequently sincerity. Real power must grow from life itself. The Buddhism of the Heian period could not continue any longer in the way it had been going; it was to become Kamakura Buddhism.

The one who struck the first note of reformation for democratic Buddhism in the Heian period was Kūya Shōnin (902–72), known as "the market sage." He left the mountains and monasteries and palatial temples and saying his Nembutsu went among the masses. He never stayed in one place,—a real wandering monk he was. Ryōnin (1072–1132) followed him but from the *Avatamsaka* (Kegon) point of view, which is founded on a philosophy of identity. Aristocracy and democracy were to be united in the Nembutsu.

The great leader of the Nembutsu was Hōnen Shōnin (1133–1212), who expounded his doctrine in numerous writings, scholarly and popular, in classical Chinese and vernacular Japanese. His teaching was simple. If we believe in Amida and his original vows (*pūrvapranidhāna*) with a devotional heart and, saying "Namu-amida-butsu" (Nembutsu), wish sincerely to be born in his Land of Purity and Happiness, we will surely be taken up by Amida and relieved of the oppressive burden of worldly cares. No elaborate ritualism, no mystifying philosophy, no labyrinthian complexity of technical terms are needed, but a simple, straightforward invocation of Amitabha Buddha—was this not a wonderful leap from the Nara and the Heian Buddhism? Hōnen's teaching is known as the Jōdo school of Buddhism.

Hōnen's worthy successor was Shinran Shōnin (1173–1262). In Shinran Pure Land Buddhism reached its culmination. In Hōnen's Nembutsu there was still something of "self-power" but in Shinran's all is given up to the "other-power," although in practice we can never get away from "self-power" as long as we are relatively-conditioned individuals. Shinran frankly admitted not only in theory but in practice that we are all sinful beings, and made no pretension to escape the outcome of his sinfulness. It is, he stated, in the very constitution of our being that we are sinful; therefore let us take refuge in the "other-power," and let alone our ignorance and sinfulness. This was, in a way, a dangerous doctrine. When it is not carefully balanced by reason and morality, it will surely turn into antinomianism. Shinran's teaching is the culmination of the Jōdo doctrine. This sect is known as the Shin sect, and, comprising millions of followers, is the most powerful in Japan.

Ippen Shōnin (1239–89) was a wandering monk like Kūya. Saying his Nembutsu and telling others to follow his example, he went around all over Japan. As he came after Hōnen and his disciples and also studied Zen, his Nembutsu has its own note. His sect never attained the popularity of the Shin or Jōdo, because he was a rolling stone which gathered no moss. He burned all his writings just before he died. What is left of them is a short collection of his letters and sayings and poems. His school is known as the Ji-shū.

One of the reasons why the Nembutsu schools prevailed

Asukaen

Wooden image of Kuya Shonin with little images of Buddha emerging from his mouth. Legend has it that the little Buddhas appeared whenever he chanted the Nembutsu. (Carved in the 13th century. Treasure of Rokuharamitsuji Temple, Kyoto City.)

Portrait of Shinran Shōnin. (Painted in *sumi* ink on paper in the 14th century. Treasure of Nishi-Honganji Temple, Kyoto City.)

Benridō

"Nichiren Shōnin Preaching." (Painted in color on silk in the 13th century. Treasure of Myōhokkeji Temple, Shizuoka Prefecture.)

Tokyo National Museum

"Honen Shōnin Preaching to His Disciples and the Villagers"—a fragment of one of the many long scrolls showing the life of Honen Shonin. (Painted in color on paper in the 14th century. Treasure of Zōjoji Temple, Tokyo.)

in this period was the idea which then gained currency, that is, the belief that the age belonged to the declining stage of Buddhism as predicted by Buddha, in which all the moral and ascetic rules given to the monks would be neglected, the people would not be wise enough to follow the profound teaching of Buddha, the monks would be quarrelsome in every way, even engaged in warfare, etc. The period just preceding the Kamakura showed every indication of this degeneracy, and wise men thought that the time had come for an entire reconstruction of Buddhism to adapt itself t⁄ the requirements of the times. They found this in the Nembutsu doctrine.

(6) Along with the Nembutsu there was another current started by Nichiren Shōnin (1222–82). Unlike most great Buddhists he rose from the lower strata of the community. His father was a fisherman in a remote village in the province of Awa (Chiba Prefecture). He exhibited his aggressive and pugnacious spirit throughout his career. His followers even now are sometimes quite militant and self-assertive.

Nichiren's teaching is founded on the *Puṇḍarīka Sūtra* (*Hokekyō*), known among Western students as the "Lotus Gospel," and may be said to be the practical application of Tendai philosophy. He believes in Śākyamuni Buddha and his eternal life, and the teaching that he did in former days on the Mount of Holy Vulture. This eternal Buddha is revealed in us who are living in this world. Amida's Pure Land is not of this world, nor is the Lotus World of Vairocana; but, says Nichiren, his Śākyamuni is here, and we are so many revelations of him. Of this revelation we become conscious when reciting "Na-mu-myō-hō-ren-ge-kyō" with singleness of purpose and sincerity of heart, as the "Myōhōrengekyō" (*Saddharma-puṇḍarīka*) has grown out of our religious yearnings. Thus, the Nichiren sect is strongly characterized by this-worldliness. Its association with the patriotic spirit is a natural consequence.

(7) The Buddhism of Kamakura was the affirmation of the religious consciousness itself against the externalism and intellectualism which characterized the Buddhism of the preceding period. It was at the same time a sort of re-assertion which consisted in the unfolding of the spiritual yearnings hitherto kept suppressed by historical conditions. Towards the end of Nara Buddhism there was a tendency to cast off all the intellectual complications which highly colored the study of Buddhism at the time, but Shingon ritualism which succeeded the Nara was too strong for this tendency to assert itself. It was not until the Kamakura period when Zen was newly introduced from China that the Japanese mind freed itself from all the external yokes which had obstructed its spontaneous growth.

There were more than twenty streams of Zen that poured into the thought realm of Buddhism from China. The aim of Zen is to throw off all the external paraphernalia which the intellect has woven around the soul and to see directly into the inmost nature of our being. Man is not a simply constructed creature; he requires many appendages, but when they grow too heavy he wants to unload himself, sometimes including his own existence.

The military class of Kamakura had a great liking for simplicity in every way: they were tired of and averse to ornate aristocracy and effeminate refinement. Zen supplied their wants to a nicety. If Shingon and Tendai were meant for the nobility and the Nembutsu for the commoner, Zen was assuredly for the soldier. Zen was in those days represented by Eisai Zenji (1141–1215) and Dōgen Zenji (1200–53).

(8) Everything that could be drawn out of Buddhism so far in the course of Japanese history unfolded itself in the Kamakura period (1192–1333), and what followed was more or less the filling-in and working-out of details. There were no more new schools possible so long as there was no new development of ideas and no shifting of values in the community where Buddhism thrived. After the Kamakura period, down to the fall of the Tokugawa Shogunate (1867), which meant roughly six hundred years of peace and uneventful life for Buddhism, there was nothing that could stimulate the growth of new life in it except that the new schools of the Kamakura period continued to flourish; more temples were built, either under the patronage of the powerful princes and lords or by the contributions of the public. And then the organizations grew stronger, the priestly hierarchy more elaborate and complicated, traditional authorities more autocratic, faith and devotion more formal, scholarship and speculation more fossilized. In other words, Buddhism was gradually losing its vitality because of the non-stimulating character of its surroundings.

The Buddhists were, however, rudely awakened from their long narcosis when the downfall of feudalism took place towards the end of the nineteenth century. Shintoism, which had been kept down under the yoke ever since the completion of the Ryōbu Shintō doctrine, shook it off by an official interference. And what may be called a mild form of persecution came over Buddhism: whatever patronage and endowments in the form of estates or donations it used to receive from the authorities, local and central, were taken away, and the temples and monasteries, including all their occupants, were thrown out into the streets, as it were, with nothing save their dreams of past comfort and prosperity.

Since then more than half a century has elapsed and Buddhists are growing more and more keenly alive to the situation; unless they meet it, there will be no choice left for them but to resign themselves to the fate of annihilation. Besides, Christianity backed by its modern methods of propaganda and its full grasp of modern ideas has been living among them for some years now. With these stimulations what Buddhism has to do is to draw more intensely and deeply than ever upon its own vital sources.

At present there are eleven sects of Buddhism in existence:

(1) Ritsu-shū (Vinaya school). It was introduced to Japan by Ganjin (Chien-chen, died 763), a Chinese priest, in 754. The Tōshōdaiji, of Nara, is its head-temple.

(2) Hossō-shū (Dharmalaksha or Vijñānamātra school). Dōshō (629–700) brought it from China in 653. There are at present three main temples in Nara belonging to this sect: Hōryūji, Kōfukuji, and Yakushiji.

(3) Kegon-shū (Avatamsaka school). Rōben (689–773) opened this sect in 740. The head-temple is Tōdaiji, Nara.

(4) Tendai-shū. The founder is Saichō (762–822), known as Dengyō Daishi, who went to China in 804 and

Tokyo National Museum

Mandala, graphic representations of the manifold figures and symbols making up the cosmic communion. (Painted in color on silk at the end of the 9th century. Treasure of Kyō-ō-gokokuji Temple, Kyoto City.)

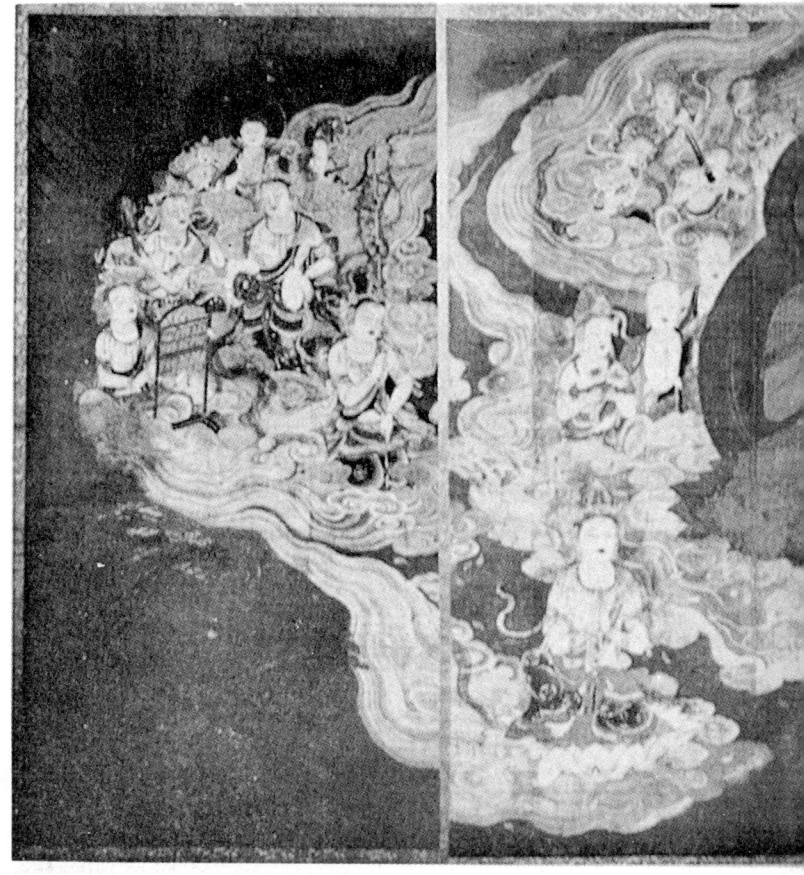

"Amida Descending to Earth to Save a Believer Who Has Chanted the Nembutsu"—a picture illustrating the Jōdo doctrine. (Painted in color on silk in the 12th century. Treasure of Daien-in Temple on Mt. Kōya, Wakayama Prefecture.)

Tokyo National Museum

The central platform for Buddhist images in the Golden Hall of the Chūsonji Temple, built in the 12th century. At Hiraizumi, Iwate Prefecture.

studied the Tendai, the Shingon, and the Zen schools of Buddhism, and came back to Japan in 805. The sect is divided into three branches whose headquarters are: Enryakuji, Onjōji, and Saikyōji, all at Ōtsu.

(5) Shingon-shū. The founder is Kūkai (774–835), known as Kōbō Daishi, who came back from China in 806 after three years' stay there. The sect is divided into two main branches, the Kogi and the Shingi, which are subdivided into eleven smaller ones. The following are the most celebrated temples of this sect: Kongōbuji, Kōya; Tōji, Kyoto; Sambōin, Kyoto; Hasedera, Hase; Chishakuin, Kyoto.

(6) Yūzūnembutsu-shū. Ryōnin (1072–1132) founded it in 1117. Its head-temple is Dainembutsuji, Osaka.

(7) Jōdo-shū. Hōnen Shōnin (1133–1212) is the father of this sect in Japan. He first proclaimed the doctrine of the Pure Land in 1125. It has two main branches, one of which is further divided into three. Chion-in, of Kyoto, is the head-temple of the more flourishing branch.

(8) Shin-shū, that is, Jōdo Shin-shū. Its founder is Shinran Shōnin (1173–1262) who, claiming that it "truly" transmits the faith and thought of his master Hōnen Shōnin, wrote the text-book of this sect in 1224. The sect is divided into ten smaller branches; the two strongest branches are the Higashi- and Nishi-Honganji, both in Kyoto, with 10,038 and 10,580 temples respectively under their jurisdiction.

(9) Zen-shū. It has two main branches, Rinzai and Sōtō. The Rinzai and the Sōtō were originally established in China: the former started with Rinzai (Lin-chi, died 867) of the T'ang dynasty and the latter with Tōzan (Tung-shan,

807–69) and his disciple Shōzan (Ts'ao-shan, 839–901), also of the T'ang. Dōgen brought the Sōtō school to Japan in 1227, whereas the Rinzai was introduced to Japan through fourteen different sources. There is a third school of Zen known as the Ōbaku, which may, however, practically be included in the Rinzai-shū. It was established in 1661 by a Chinese Zen-master, Ingen (1592–1673). The Mampukuji, of Uji, which is built in the Chinese style, is its main temple. The Sōtō-shū has two main temples: Eiheiji near Fukui and Sōjiji at Tsurumi. The Rinzai has fourteen, of which Myōshinji in Kyoto is the largest.

(10) Nichiren-shū. Nichiren Shōnin (1222–82), who first proclaimed its teaching in 1253, is its founder. It is divided into two schools, which are further divided into nine, and the largest and most influential of them all is known as the Nichiren-shū, bearing the original title unchanged. The head-temple of the Nichiren-shū is Kuonji at Minobu.

(11) Ji-shū. This was established by Ippen Shōnin (1239–89) in 1276, and its head-temple is the Shōjōkōji, popularly known as Yugyōdera, in Fujisawa, Kanagawa Prefecture.

The eleven sects of Buddhism at present, with the numbers of their temples and adherents, are as follows:

	Temples	Adherents
Ritsu-shū	37	11,878
Hossō-shū	283	174,400
Kegon-shū	158	57,620

	Temples	Adherents
Tendai-shū	5,498	2,141,502
Shingon-shū	19,462	7,530,531
Yūzūnembutsu-shū	362	101,106
Jōdo-shū	8,317	4,231,342
Shin-shū	21,852	9,007,582
Zen-shū ⎰ Sōtō	15,190	6,669,070
⎱ Rinzai	5,966	2,983,727
Ōbaku	503	166,540
Nichiren-shū	8,952	9,120,028
Ji-shū	426	40,349
Total	87,006	42,540,325

Source: Religious Affairs Section, Research Bureau, Ministry of Education. (As of December 31, 1956.)

III

SOME EMINENT PERSONS IN JAPANESE BUDDHISM

The worth of a religion is judged by the highest personalities it produces; they are generally above the institutions whose creators they once were. When such institutions pass the stage of maturity and become a secular or political power, they degenerate and turn into a nursery of paupers and charlatans and the whole thing becomes a mockery. No religion is to be judged by this. Besides the founders of sects already mentioned in the preceding chapter, the following Buddhists among many others deserve special mention here.

Gyōgi Bosatsu (668–749)

While the Emperor Shōmu (reigned 724–49) was mobilizing all his economic and political and religious forces towards the erection of the Tōdaiji and other temples all over the country, and while the Buddhist doctors and philosophers were busily occupied with the study and exposition of the texts brought by their brother-monks from China, there were some Buddhists who might not have been so brilliant in scholarly attainment but who really took to heart the practical demonstration of the teaching of their predecessors in the faith. Among such, Gyōgi was the most prominent. He himself was a great scholar of the Vijñāna-mātra school of Mahayana Buddhism, but he was by no means satisfied with an achievement of this sort. He wished to propagate or rather practice his Buddhism among the masses. He wanted them to share his spiritual attainments, whatever they were. He wanted his fellow-beings, who were not so fortunate as he and his scholarly friends, to be well taught in the Buddhist doctrine and to master it with all its technical intricacies. With this in view he seems to have initiated them into the faith of the Pure Land. His followers increased so rapidly in numbers and power that the authorities became somewhat apprehensive of the movement, as they thought it might lead to political or social complications. This was, however, an altogether unnecessary worry on the part of the officialdom of the time. Gyōgi went all over Japan helping the people in practical ways: by building bridges, opening highways and hot springs, establishing ports for seafarers, digging wells and canals, constructing burial grounds, erecting temples where the Buddhist images carved by himself were enshrined, and so on. His memory still lives even among people living in the remoter parts of the country.

Gyōgi was also of great spiritual help in the erection of the Tōdaiji, designed by the Emperor Shōmu. The latter with all his political powers could not bring such a gigantic and really epoch-making undertaking as this to a successful completion without someone spiritually inspiring, not only to the Emperor but also to the masses, who were also concerned with the enterprise. It must not be forgotten in this connection that women, too, were quite active in keeping up popular interest in the affair and also in Buddhism generally; for it was they who looked after the sick, the hungry, and the poor, and contributed largely to the erection of the subsidiary statues in the group around the Great Buddha (Daibutsu) at the Tōdaiji.

Kōshō Bosatsu, or Eison (1202–90), and Ninshō Bosatsu, or Ryōkan (1217–1303)

These two monks, belonging to the Vinaya school of Buddhism, may be mentioned together. They are both titled "Bosatsu," i.e., Bodhisattva, which was the title given by the Court because of their philanthropic undertakings and exhibitions of the truly Buddhist spirit. Ninshō was ordained by Kōshō, and it is very likely that the latter inspired the former in his *dāna-pāramitā* (charity) activities.

Kōshō was a great devotee of the Vinaya, for he believed that no one could be a good honest Buddhist monk unless he was a zealous observer of the Vinaya rules as instituted by Buddha himself. It was he, indeed, who resuscitated the Vinaya school in the Kamakura period (1192–1333). He also took an active or rather a spiritual part at the time of the Mongolian invasion in 1281, when he was ordered by the Court to offer prayers at the Shintō shrine of Yawata in the province of Yamato. The gale, it was said, which destroyed the Mongolian fleet off Kyūshū was attributable to his prayers. The Emperor Gouda was very pleased with him and asked how he could be rewarded for his spiritual achievement. The monk's reply was: "Please let *saké* drinking be stopped for three days all over the country."

Many members of the Imperial Court, including ex-emperors, empresses, the court ladies, and nobles vied indeed one with another to receive the Buddhist precepts from him. He, however, did not think very much of the

Imperial favors showered upon him; he remembered more the sufferings undergone in various ways by the multitudes. He had an image of Mañjuśri (Monju in Japanese) enshrined at every place where beggars and outcasts were gathered; for, according to a Buddhist legend, the Bodhisattva Mañjuśri is said to incarnate himself in the form of a member of the despised class of people so as to make them think of the laws of moral causation. Kōshō also helped them in material ways by giving them money and rice whenever possible. Being a poor monk himself he had no resources of his own, but rich people were glad to give him more than enough for his personal needs—indeed very much more, so that he used them freely for distribution among the needy. He never went out on special tours to solicit alms, for a forced donation was a defiled one, he thought.

Ninshō Bosatsu, also known as Ryōkan Bō, was a worthy successor to Kōshō. While living at the Saidaiji, Nara, he made it his mission to work as an ordinary laborer at the laundry and lavatory belonging to the monastery. He also had dispensaries and other charitable establishments, where unfortunate people were cared for, and put in good order. In 1252 he went to Kamakura, where a scion of the Hōjō family had their family temple (called Gokurakuji) renovated for the residence of Ninshō, who stayed there for a long time. According to record, he built 189 bridges, opened 71 highways, dug 33 wells, established 5 bathhouses for the needy, and also had a hospital in Kamakura where during his twenty years of charitable activities it is recorded that the number of inmates cared for amounted to 57,250, of whom

46,800 were restored to health and left the establishment. He, as well as Kōshō, looked after animals well: he built hospitals for sick horses and kennels for dogs. People followed him as the god of medicine.

The establishment of bathhouses generally was one of the Buddhist practical activities. At the temples a warm bath was made twice a month and all the monks bathed in it. The Zen monastery has a bathhouse among its regular establishments. The bathhouse at the Tōji, of Kyoto, is one with special architectural interest, and is now under national protection.

The Empress Kōmyō (701–60) of the Nara period, according to a Buddhist history called *Genkō Shakusho*, built a bathhouse where she vowed she would personally wash one thousand beggars. The last one who came to be looked after by the Imperial bathroom attendant was a horrible-looking leper. She hesitated, but thinking of her vow she went on with her self-imposed work. After finishing her most disagreeable task, she told him not to breathe a word about it to others—when lo! the man was seen emitting rays of light from every pore of his skin and he said to the Empress: "I am no other personage than the Buddha Akṣobhya himself (Ashuku in Japanese). Do not let others know that you saw me."

At this memorable spot she later erected a temple for Akṣobhya. This spot is identified with a district now known as Kitayama, or Higashi-no-saka, in the northern part of Nara. It seems to have been a kind of quarantine for lepers in ancient days, and Ninshō Bosatsu had his establishment here. While at the Saidaiji, which was about five miles from

Tokyo National Museum

Wooden image of Gyōgi Bosatsu. (Carved in the 13th century. Treasure of Saidaiji Temple, Nara City.)

Portrait of Kōshō Bosatsu. (Painted in color on silk in the 13th century. Treasure of Shin-Daibutsuji Temple, Mie Prefecture.)

"Myōe Shōnin Practicing *Zazen* in a Tree." (Painted in color on silk in the 13th century. Treasure of Kozanji Temple, Kyoto City.)

Tokyo National Museum

"Kanzan Kokushi," by Hakuin. (Painted in color on paper. Owned by Mr. Moritatsu Hosokawa.)

Japan Travel Bureau

Kitayama, he walked every other day to take some of the crippled patients on his own shoulders to the city where they could beg food.

Myōe Shōnin (1163–1232)

Another illuminating star composing the galaxy of Buddhists of the Kamakura period was Myōe. He was a great friend and teacher of Yasutoki Hōjō, who was an influential power in the government at the time. That the Hōjō régime is noted for its wise administration, as is recognized by all historians, was due largely to the spiritual influence exercised by Myōe Shōnin.

The temple where he spent most of his time and in fact passed his last moments was the Kōzanji, which is still in existence—one of the sites most reputed for maple tints in the vicinity of Kyoto. When his fame reached the Court, the Empress Kenreimon-in wished to receive the Precepts from Myōe Shōnin. He was invited to the Imperial palace. The Empress sat behind the screen on a higher seat at a distance and requested him to perform the Precepts-giving Ceremony for her. This was in opposition to his idea of the spiritual dignity of a Buddhist monk. He said, "As a subject of the Empress I am of low birth; but here I am before your Majesty as a spiritual teacher whose whole life has been devoted to the understanding and practice of things not of this world. Mine is not to bow even before the gods. If my seat is lower than yours in my capacity as performer of the Precepts-giving Rite, both you and I shall be committing a grave offence against the spiritual law. I say this for the sake of things far higher than any worldly considerations." So saying, the Shōnin began to leave the room. The Empress was taken aback, and coming out from behind the screen asked for his forgiveness. This incident is said to have cemented their spiritual friendship, which continued till the end of his life.

In his ordinary life, however, Myōe's attitude towards all things was friendliness itself. According to his biographer, he cherished the *Avatamsaka* (Kegon) idea that all beings are endowed with Buddha-nature, including ants, beasts, birds, and all other animals. When he passed by a dog lying down or a horse or an ox at work, bowing to it as if it were a good friend of his, he greeted it kindly.

When Yasutoki Hōjō came up to Kyoto as commander of his army, some of the Kyoto forces who fought against him fled from the capital and were reported to have found a refuge at Kōzanji, the temple of Myōe Shōnin. One of Yasutoki's generals arrested the latter and brought him before the commander for examination. When Yasutoki saw the Shōnin and listened to the announcement of the general, he hastily came down from his seat and respectfully requested the Shōnin to take the seat of honor. The Shōnin then said that, from his Buddhist point of view, both friends and foes were equally objects of reverence and kindly considerations, and that whenever they came to him for protection he was ready to help them regardless of their political allegiance, and that if this went against the policy of the commander of Hōjō forces, he was prepared at any moment to surrender himself into the hands of the prosecutor.

Yasutoki was greatly impressed with the humanitarian feelings and noble attitude of this really saintly Buddhist

monk, and sincerely apologized to him for the thoughtless-
ness of his general. He then expressed his deep regrets for
not having had a good opportunity before this for an inter-
view with Myōe in more appropriate surroundings; but he
was glad that he had now made his acquaintance, anyhow,
and would look for another occasion to see him again when
he was relieved of the pressing business at hand. It was in
this way that his friendship with the Shōnin started and it
was kept up ever afterwards. He was truly a great and worthy
disciple of this remarkable Buddhist monk who flourished
in the earlier part of the Hōjō régime.

I may add one more anecdote in the life of Myōe
Shōnin which illustrates his view of prayer. When some
one asked him to offer to Buddha a special prayer for his
own benefit, the Shōnin said: "I pray every morning and
every evening for the sake of all beings and I am sure
you are also included among them as one of the sentient
beings. There is no special need to offer a prayer for one
single particular person. If your wish is something to be
granted in the general scheme of things it will most assuredly
be granted; but if not, even with the power of Buddha,
nothing can be done for you."

Daitō Kokushi (1282–1337) and
Kanzan Kokushi (1277–1360)

These two great Zen masters of Japan may best be treated
here conjointly, for they, together with Daiō Kokushi (or
Shōmyō, 1235–1308), who was teacher of Daito, are known
as fathers of the Japanese Rinzai school of Zen Buddhism.

Daitō Kokushi, Kanzan's teacher, was patronized and

revered by the Emperor Godaigo (1288–1339), for the Emperor himself was a great student of Zen. When the Kokushi had his audience with the Emperor, the latter remarked, "Wonderful that a Buddhist monk stands before an Imperial personage!" Kokushi lost no time in replying, "Wonderful that an Imperial personage stands before a Buddhist monk!" Another time the Emperor asked, "Who is he who finds no companionship among all beings?" The Kokushi, moving the fan in his hand, said, "The Imperial breeze like the fan gently moves over all beings [to make them grow]."

The Buddhist scholars of the time, who were much given to the intellectual understanding of the Sūtras, did not like the way the Zen masters were in favor at the Court, and proposed to have an open discussion with them in the presence of the Emperor. This was granted on the condition that those who were defeated would become disciples to the victor. When the day came a scholar of great reputation appeared and opened the forum: "What is Zen that it should claim a special transmission outside the scriptural teaching?" To this Daitō Kokushi answered, "A hexagonal grindstone runs through vacuity." The questioner was nonplussed. Another learned doctor came forward with a box. Seeing it, Daitō asked, "What is your box?" The doctor answered, "This is the box in which the whole universe is packed up." The Kokushi raised the short stick which was in his hand and striking the box broke it to pieces. He said, "How will it be when the universe is broken up?" The doctors did not know what to do with this Zen monk whose language and behavior were more than they could cope with.

125

Tokyo National Museum

(Above) The gorgeously decorated metal sutra box for holding
the 33 volumes of Buddhist sutras dedicated to the Itsukushima
Shrine by the Heike family in the 12th century; (below right)
two of the sūtra scrolls from the collection, and (below left)
the inside of one of the volumes. (All treasures of Itsukushima
Shrine, Hiroshima Prefecture.)

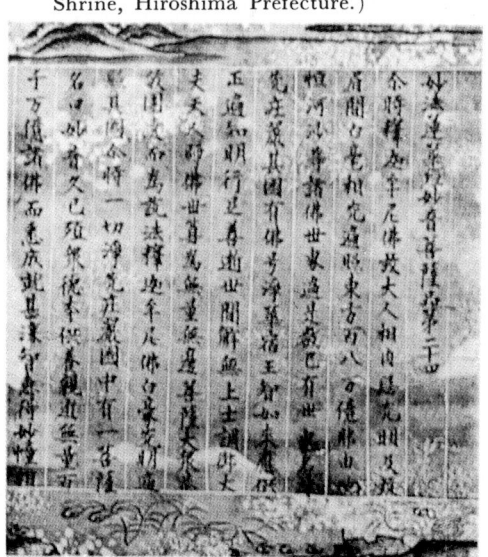

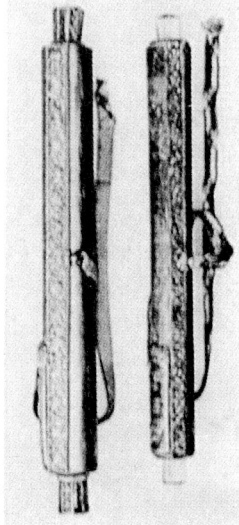

(Above left) *Sharitō*, pagoda-shaped reliquary, made in the 13th century. (Treasure of Saidaiji Temple, Nara Prefecture.) (Below right) A group of altar instruments, symbolizing the Buddhist world, used in the Esoteric Buddhist service. (Made in the 12th century. Treasure of Itsukushima Shrine, Hiroshima Prefecture.) (Below left) A *Keman* (wreath of flowers), an ornament hung in a temple altar. (Treasure of Chūsonji Temple, Hiraizumi, Iwate Prefecture.)

Tokyo National Museum

When Daitō was about to pass away in 1337, the Emperor asked him about his successor, and he recommended Kanzan as a worthy one. But he added that, being an extraordinary character, Kanzan might be difficult to locate and even when located might be hard to be persuaded to appear in the world. Daitō went on, "If, however, he is told of Daitō's death he might be induced to come to the capital." After many vain searches, Kanzan was finally discovered in the province of Mino far away from the crowded towns. Driving an ox or pulling a cart for them, he was with the poor peasants. At first he refused to betray his identity and showed no inclination to leave his humble friends. But when the Imperial messenger told him about the passing of his teacher, Daitō Kokushi, he finally yielded.

Kanzan now became the founder of the Myōshinji, which is at present one of the most flourishing temples in Japan. In the beginning, however, it was far from being a present-able structure although it was one of the Imperial detached palaces. He had no idea of improving it. When he was not occupied with interviewing his pupils he himself was found sweeping the temple grounds. One of his lay relatives once paid him a visit, and seeing how badly his residence needed repairs, he proposed to pay the expenses for them. This irritated the master very much. He roared, "You worldly fellow! It is none of your business to be concerned with my house. When you have finished seeing me about the Dharma, make haste and begone!"

His temple, however, apparently required renovation. When the roof leaked badly, he called out to his attendants to bring something for the dripping rain. One of them hurriedly ran out and brought him a bamboo basket, which pleased him greatly, while another monk who spent some time in finding and bringing a proper vessel was strongly reprimanded.

The Kokushi's way of dealing with his pupils was thus always characterized with the straightforwardness of Zen. When there was no more fuel to make a bath for a visitor, he ordered a part of his temple to be destroyed until enough fuel was gathered for the purpose. When a monk came to see him, he asked, "What are you here for?" The monk replied, "I have a matter of great concern about which I wish your instruction." "What is it?" "The business of birth-and-death." Kanzan roared, "Here is no birth-and-death. Begone!" The Zen monk's personality often presents an unexpected characteristic which is altogether missing in other Buddhists of high scholarship and piety.

Before Kanzan came to Kyoto to study Zen under Daitō, he was first ordained as a Zen monk at the Kenchōji, Kamakura. It was not until he was thirty years old that he showed marked personality as a Zen student. Once when he learned that there was a great Zen master at the Daitokuji, he could not wait even for another day; he started right away for Kyoto. It is said that on the way along the Tōkaidō highway he never once stopped to look at Mt. Fuji though it must have taken him at least two or three days to pass the sight of the most beautiful mountain of Japan. When he reached Daitokuji, the master, Daitō Kokushi, demanded an introductory letter, but to this he defiantly replied, "Every great teacher of Zen knows who his visitors are as soon as they cross the threshold of his room, and you as one ought to be able to recognize what kind of man I am."

When he knew that he was about to die, he said to his chief disciple, "I am going to travel presently; please get me my traveling hat." With this, he took the disciple with him as far as a tree by the pond, where he bade farewell: "You are the only person who knows of my departure. After me, you will exercise yourself for the cultivation of the Zen spirit in this country." Resting himself on the staff he carried, he passed away.

Incidentally, it may be remarked that there were many Zen monks who died in an unconventional manner. Daitō Kokushi was lame of a leg, and had some difficulty in sitting properly cross-legged. When his death approached he mounted the chair in which he wished to sit, but as his leg was not obedient to his will, he forced it with a crack, the blood staining his robe. He said, "As I have been obedient to you all my life, you obey me at this last moment for once." He then quietly wrote his farewell poem and passed away.

IV

BUDDHISM AND JAPANESE CULTURE

Buddhism has had a great deal to do not only with the development of the arts in Japan, but with the advancement of culture in all its branches. In fact Japan without Buddhism would probably never have reached its present stage of enlightenment. Buddhism represents so far in the history of Japan almost everything she stands for. It was through its agency that this isolated island of the Far East got acquainted with continental thought and civilization, Indian and Chinese, upon which our ancestors built the foundation of present-day Japan.

As to the arts, as is well known, they are inseparable from Buddhism. Visit the Hōryūji near Nara and you will find it a regular treasure house of the arts. The grand ensemble of architecture alone, not to speak of the wall-paintings* and sculptures, all of which are great works of art, is a most remarkable monument to the Buddhist genius. In the Heian (784–1192), Kamakura (1192–1333), and Muromachi (1392–1573) periods which followed, almost all the masterpieces of art are directly or indirectly related to Buddhism. Any historical Buddhist temple in Kyoto and vicinity is a real repository of the artistic works created by Japanese

---

* Soon after the war these fresco pictures were destroyed, most unfortunately, by fire. The loss is irreparable.

men of genius, whose sources of imagination and inspiration may invariably be traced back to Buddhism.

In India, as we know, religion and philosophy are so inextricably interwoven that it is impossible to differentiate the one from the other. In the Buddhism which grew up in India, we find intellect and intuition closely knitted together. Religious imagination helps to create art, while religious intuition proves to be a great stimulation to rationalization. While intuition is opposed in some way to rationalization, the latter is really rooted in the former and separates itself only when conditions demand it. This is one of the reasons why Buddhism is more intellectually disposed than any other religious system in the world, and primitive Buddhism has often been regarded as an ethical movement. The Japanese mind thus nourished in this atmosphere has grown up to handle understandingly any philosophical thought which might reach this shore from anywhere else. The doctrine of absolute identity or of cosmic interrelationship elaborated in the Kegon philosophy is the outcome of Buddhist intuitions. Professional philosophers may work on them and present them more analytically and develop them into forms of dialectics. Fundamentally, Buddhist intuitions are some of the deepest the human mind has so far realized. The Japanese have been trained in them for the last one thousand years.

Some foreign critics hold that the Japanese mind is not philosophical. While it is difficult to know exactly what they mean by this statement, the Japanese and the Chinese people are certainly not so abstractly-minded or intellectually-addicted as some European minds are. But in some ways the

Oriental mentality goes deeper into the perception of reality, for reality when conceptualized ceases to be itself—it is to be taken hold of concretely in its suchness. Buddhist thought, inasmuch as it is Indian, is full of abstractions, but when it reached Japan after going through the Chinese crucible of concrete thinking and practical living, it dropped much of its other-worldly aloofness and transcendental unapproachability and merged itself into the people's everyday life. The art of tea is one of such instances. What Western mind would ever attempt to find its philosophy in the tea-cup and the drinking of the yellowish beverage? Poets may take themselves to wine but not to tea.

There is one thing at least in the history of Japanese Buddhism which any writer on the subject must not ignore, —its influence on Bushidō, "the Way of the Warrior." It may be better to say the Zen Buddhist influence, for it is chiefly Zen that was studied by the samurai class. The reason is that the samurai was always facing death as it might befall him at any moment. Though this is the case with everybody, it was most keenly felt by the samurai, whose life in the feudal days was constantly exposed to dangers, as he was a soldier, a policeman, a statesman, and generally a guardian of peace. He used to carry two swords, one short and the other long, and he was to be ready at any moment to make use of them and to be responsible for the outcome. The most efficient and capable samurai was, therefore, the one who would not hesitate to sacrifice his life when the occasion called for it. But this defying death was not to be just giving up one's life after the fashion of a desperado. There ought to be a certain philosophical under-

standing of the question, "What is life?" or "What is death?"
This understanding is given by Zen simply and directly, that
is, without the intricate medium of intellection or ritualism,
—which excellently suited the samurai psychology.

The samurai might be a great statesman, or a learned
scholar, but the one virtue most needed for him was to be
decisive and not flinching before dangers. It was only when
this state of mind was realized that he could carry on his
profession satisfactorily, regardless of any personal consequence that might follow from it. In other words, whatever
decision he came to would thus be executed in an impersonal fashion and therefore to the point.

Bushidō developed under the Hōjō régime when Zen
Buddhism was introduced from China, and it was at once
embraced by the Hōjō family and their retainers. They were
noted for their simple life, bravery, and wise administration.
The Mongolian invasions in the years 1274 and 1281, which
were, indeed, the greatest events in the history of Japan
before the Russo-Japanese War (1904–5), were repulsed by
them, and most historians think the strength of character
of the central figure engaged in the task was derived from
his training in Zen. However this may be, there is no doubt
that Zen has been a great spiritual force for the building
up of Japanese Bushidō.

Among the most important contributions Buddhism has
given to the moral and spiritual culture of the Japanese
people, we may mention the spirit of tolerance and the love
of nature. The first appears to be a kind of spiritual love for
the enemy. After the Mongolian invaders were driven back,
for which many sacrificed their lives on both sides, a temple

(Engakuji, 1282) was erected at Kamakura (now Kita-Kamakura) for the consolation of the departed spirits, Japanese and Mongolian. At the termination of the Korean War undertaken by Taikō Hideyoshi in 1591–8, one monument was erected in Korea itself and another at Mount Kōya, both of which were dedicated to the dead on both sides, Japanese and Korean, with the prayer that they would all attain Buddhahood regardless of the sides they represented. Death wipes out all such earthly considerations and unites every one of us in one Reality, that is, in one Buddhahood.

With the decline of feudalism under the impact of Western civilization late in the nineteenth century, it was inevitable for Bushidō to lose much of its old spirit, good as well as bad. "Modern" Japan is bent upon the pursuit of happiness and the raising of standards of living mostly on the materialistic side of human existence. It has almost forgotten the old samurai ideals of virility and simplicity and artistic appreciation. This is what is known as the Westernization and industrialization of "the backward, underdeveloped East."

The love of Nature, which is innate to the Japanese heart, has been enhanced and given a far deeper significance by Buddhism. What was mere sensitivity before the introduction of Buddhism has lent itself to a spiritual interpretation under Buddhist influence; what was no more than a naïve sentimental response to Nature became identified with the most comprehensive and highly religious feeling for it, animate and inanimate. *Kuyō* (*pūja* in Sanskrit) is one of the manifestations of such feeling. *Pūja* originally means

Bronze images of Śakyamuni and his attendants enshrined in the Main Hall of the Hōryūji Temple, Nara Prefecture. (Cast in the 7th century.)

Wooden image of Miroku Bosatsu (*Maitreya*) carved from a single block of wood in the 7th century. (Treasure of Kōryūji Temple, Kyoto City.)

Tokyo National Museum

Amida and his attendants. (Cast in bronze in the 8th century. Treasure of Hōryūji Temple, Nara Prefecture.)

Benrido

Bronze image of Amida, chief object of worship in the Amida
Hall of the Byōdōin Temple in the southeastern suburbs of Kyoto
City. (Cast in the 12th century.)

Wooden image of Kichijoten. (Carved in the 12th century. Treasure of Jōruriji Temple, Kyoto Prefecture.)

Benridō

Wooden image of Jizō Bosatsu, carved by Kaikei, renowned sculptor of the 13th century. (Treasure of Tōdaiji Temple, Nara City.)

Asukaen

"reverence," "paying homage," or "adoration." This is given both to persons and non-sentient objects. When it is applied to a person nowadays in Japanese Buddhism, it is making offerings, in most cases material. When it is done to other beings, including dead objects and even man-made instruments, it is the sentiment of love expressed in a peculiarly Buddhist form. We often hear or read about a *kuyō* rite performed for the insects singing in the autumn field, or the brushes thrown away by the painter and calligrapher, or the needles used by tailors and housekeeping wives, or the broken tools, or the human or animal corpses used for medical experiments, or the fishes caught in the fishermen's nets, the animals killed by butchers, the enemies fallen in the battlefield, the animals which died in captivity, for instance in the zoological gardens, or the plants weeded on the farm for the sake of the stronger ones, and many other objects of nature or of human construction. To understand this strange Buddhist performance, one must be thoroughly acquainted with the Mahayana feeling of universal salvation and cosmic fellowship, which is no more than the feeling of love for all things sentient and non-sentient.

The idea of conquering Nature is something quite foreign to the Oriental, especially the Buddhist, way of thinking. The Japanese people never think of subduing Nature to their will. For to them Nature is something to revere or to admire, or to love, and generally to be on terms of friendship with. The idea of conquest was imported from the West. Buddhism never thinks of turning Nature to human service. Even when vegetables are picked, cooked, and consumed, even when cotton is gathered, spun, and woven for dresses of all kinds, we never think of having subdued them, we are sincerely thankful for the service Nature is willing to give us. The Buddhist ritual of *kuyō* illustrates the feeling Buddhists have for objects of Nature generally. They never think of subjugating Nature or of making her serve them in the fashion of a handmaid. If they were to climb a high mountain, they would make offerings to it in order to express their feeling of respect for its spirit, whatever it may be. If they were to release the energy deeply hidden in the atom, they would never say, "We have conquered it," but they would thank Nature for revealing her secrets in response to our prayers rendered in the form of "experiments." They would not think of turning these secrets into instruments for slaughtering their fellow-beings by hundreds of thousands. They, rather, would immediately try to use the energy for increasing the mutual happiness of humanity.

Suggestions for Further Reading

Part One, Zen Buddhism

There are not many books on Zen in English, in fact, in any of the European languages. We must go to the original sources for information, but as these are either in Chinese or Japanese, they are not accessible to the general reader. The following books, most of which are by the present author, are recommended.

Barrett, William: *Zen Buddhism.* New York: Doubleday & Co., 1956. (This was compiled by Dr. Barrett from Suzuki's various works on Zen, and appeared as one of the Doubleday Anchor Books.)

Sasaki, Ruth F.: *Development of Chinese Zen after the Sixth Patriarch.* New York: The Zen Institute of America, Inc., 1955. (This is an English translation from the original German treatise by Heinrich Dumoulin, with notes and other informing material.)

The following four books are by D. T. Suzuki, published by Rider & Co., London, 1949–1955:

Introduction to Zen Buddhism.

Living by Zen.

Manual of Zen Buddhism.

Studies in Zen Buddhism.

There is another book by D. T. Suzuki soon to be published, probably in the fall of 1958, by Pantheon, New York. It bears the title: *Zen and Japanese Culture.*

Part Two, Japanese Buddhism

Benedict, Ruth: *The Chrysanthemum and the Sword.* Rutland, Vermont: Charles E. Tuttle Co., 1954.

Burtt, E. A.: *The Teachings of the Compassionate Buddha.* New York: The New American Library (Mentor Books), 1955.

Conze, Edward: *Buddhism.* Oxford: Bruno Cassirer, 1951.

Eliot, Sir Charles: *Japanese Buddhism.* London: Edward Arnold & Co., 1935.

Humphreys, Christmas: *Buddhism.* Middlesex: Penguin Books, 1952.

Morgan, Kenneth W.: *The Path of the Buddha, Buddhism Interpreted by Buddhists.* New York: Ronald Press Co., 1956.

Sansom, Sir George: *Japan, a Short Cultural History.* New York: Appleton Century Co., 1943.

Suzuki, Beatrice L.: *Mahayana Buddhism, a Brief Outline.* London: David Marlowe, Ltd., 1948.

INDEX

The figures refer to the pages, those in heavy type indicating information in fuller detail. The capital letters, J. C. & S., within the brackets stand for Japanese, Chinese and Sanskrit.

IN ENGLISH

IN SANSKRIT

IN JAPANESE

148

IN CHINESE